THE CHRISTIAN CHURCH
AND THE
OLD TESTAMENT

THE CHRISTIAN CHURCH
AND
THE OLD TESTAMENT

by
ARNOLD A. VAN RULER

Translated by Geoffrey W. Bromiley

WILLIAM B. EERDMANS PUBLISHING COMPANY
Grand Rapids, Michigan

Translated from the German *Die christliche Kirche und das Alte Testament,* published by Kaiser Verlag, Munich, Germany, 1955.

PREFACE

The work of A. A. van Ruler is not as widely known in the English-speaking world as it deserves. It is thus a particular pleasure to make this small but significant example available to a wider public.

The theme is a crucial one in the modern hermeneutical debate, for in tackling the understanding and use of the Old Testament in the Christian Church van Ruler necessarily becomes involved in weighty ecclesiastical, biblical, and dogmatic themes, e.g., the status of Israel today, the unity and inter-relation of the Testaments, and the function of Jesus Christ within the total purpose and work of the Trinity.

Special features of the study are the acuteness of the questioning, the penetration in criticism of various current and popular solutions, the awareness of ultimate theological issues, and the originality of the thesis which, even if only sketchily and not wholly convincingly, van Ruler himself advances.

To make the reader's task a little less difficult, some of the lengthier footnotes have been brought into the main body of the text as small-print sections. Apart from this, however, the original is given unaltered as well as unabridged.

Geoffrey W. Bromiley

Pasadena, California, Trinity, 1971

H2801

CONTENTS

INTRODUCTION

This book is an attempt to answer the question, How does the Christian church evaluate and use the Old Testament? — a question that has a fundamental bearing on theology, according to L. Goppelt. "In my age," he writes, "the understanding and interpretation of the Old Testament are very closely correlated with the basic theological position."[1] Our basic theological position will decide our attitude toward the Old Testament, and at the same time our attitude toward the Old Testament will help to determine our general theological position.

Let us be clear that we are not talking here about what is thought in many circles to be the crux of one's basic theological position — the problem of the Scripture principle. The point at issue when we ask about the Old Testament is far more than the authority of Holy Scripture, to which one either does or does not submit. In fact, this formal question of the Scripture principle is child's play compared to the practical, substantive question of *how* we should acknowledge the authority of the Old Testament as canonical Scripture, the Word of God. The difficulties the modern age has with the Scripture principle as such have been felt by the Christian church since the first century as far as the Old Testament is concerned. The primitive church had to claim the Old Testament, if only to validate itself as being in the will of God. But what was the church really to make of the Old Testament? And what *has* it made of it?[2] How much of it has been set aside so that we are no longer subject to it?

One might point out that Jesus was very closely bound to the OT and knew no other God than the God of the OT. This argument is decisive for F. W. A. Korff; *Christologie*, II, 16ff. According to H. Bornkamm, "the New Testament's use of the Old really precluded the church from rejecting the latter altogether"; *Luther und das AT,* p. 210; Eng. tr., p. 248.

Adolf Harnack's well-known thesis that "to reject the Old Testament in the second century was an error the church rightly resisted; to maintain it in the sixteenth century was a destiny the Reformation could not escape; but still to preserve it in the nineteenth century as one of the canonical documents of Protestantism is the result of religious and ecclesiastical paralysis" (*Marcion,* p. 217), throws great light on the main points in the history of the problem. Like many of Harnack's other theses, it gives the systematic theologian much to think about. Did the Reformers adopt the Scripture principle too hastily in their dogmatic consolidation? Did they take over the OT without sufficient reflection? On what grounds did they assume that the cultic and civil legislation of the OT has been done away with, at least in the literal sense? Lutheran theologians could properly ask whether it was not the moral law that has been abolished according to Paul. For Roman Catholic theology, which recognizes tradition and the teaching office as well as Scripture, such questions about the OT are not nearly so pressing as they are for Protestantism.

No matter how great the difficulties in answering questions about the church's use of the Old Testament, these questions are, at a central point, decisive. How we answer them decides how we understand Jesus Christ in his historical character, his Jewish context, and his divine validation. It decides the church's view of itself as the church of God,[3] as an element in the *mystérion* of God's saving action in history. It decides our interpretation of the salvation given us in Jesus Christ, and in that connection our estimate of earthly and temporal life and of the whole structure of Christian existence. It concerns equally the matter of the apostolate and the elements of Christianization in it, not to mention the basic question of the apostolate: the relation of the church of Jesus Christ to the chosen people of Israel.[4] Our whole understanding of the kingdom of God — and therefore also of the catholicity of the Christian faith, the Christian church, and Christianity — is determined by what we think of the Old Testament and how we handle it.

Bearing all this in mind, we can shoulder the difficulties of this problem without trying to oversimplify it. As I see it, the apostolic council whose deliberations are recorded in Acts 15 was already unable to master this problem. Paul and the other writers of the New Testament had very different estimates of the Old Testament and used it in very different ways.[5] And it would seem to me that in no age — not even in the age of the Reformation — has the church really known what God intended for the Old Testament in the Christian situation and what the church itself should do with it. Reformed theology since Calvin (except for Cocceius, with his Christology of salvation realism) has usually taken a positive view of the Old Testament and treated it literally. Now, in the twentieth century, we need to explore the whole problem anew from the standpoint of systematic theology on the basis of the findings of historico-critical investigation.

On the one hand I do not think that it is permissible in the Christian church to condemn a whole century — in this case the nineteenth — for this would not be in keeping with the spiritual nature of love. On the other hand, I believe that historico-critical investigation has enabled us to see for the first time what the basic principle of the Reformation — that only the literal sense of God's written Word can save — really means when applied to the OT. In this respect, too, the modern age is a child of the Reformation.

We may roughly sketch current views of the Old Testament as follows:

(1) The standpoint that disparages the Old Testament completely. The Old Testament is either lumped with paganism (as by Schleiermacher)[6] or seen at best only in contrast with the New Testament (as by Hirsch).[7]   A much cruder form of this view was expressed in the sixteenth century: Calvin talks about the views of Servetus and certain Anabaptists, who regarded the people of Israel as a "herd of swine" "fattened by the Lord on this earth without any hope of heavenly immortality."[8]

(2) The standpoint that interprets the Old Testament as no more than a history of failure. It is prophetically significant in the New Testament age because the Christian continually sees himself in this history of failure to the extent that he stands in

unbelief.[9] Baumgärtel speaks in terms similar to these, although he places more emphasis on the alien character of Old Testament religion as compared with the gospel.[10]

(3) The standpoint that parallels pagan religion, philosophy, mysticism, and speculation with the Old Testament, and regards both realms as preparation for the supreme revelation in Christ.[11] The merit of this view is that it puts the question whether the final evaluation of paganism might not be positive.[12]

(4) The standpoint that sees the Old Testament as indispensable for understanding the New Testament in its historical sense. This view is unquestionably right. The church must take it seriously, from the theological aspect too, although the question arises whether this consideration can have the last word in the church, or at least whether it can establish the canonicity of the Old Testament in the Christian church.

E. Sellin rightly points out that it is historical criticism that, in the face of both Schleiermacher and the Enlightenment, has referred to the "unbreakable bond," "which exists in history between the Old Testament and the gospel of Jesus and the apostles"; *Die Religion in Geschichte und Gegenwart*, I[2], 984.

(5) The standpoint that argues for a consistent theological estimate of the Old Testament, even in Christian theology. The Old Testament is an independent source of knowledge and piety, with a distinctive message even for the present generation. This is the point of view of many Old Testament scholars, especially those controlled by the Lutheran dialectic of law and gospel (among them A. H. Edelkoort, H. Wheeler Robinson, and H. H. Rowley).

(6) The standpoint that regards the Old Testament as a providential preparation in earthly history for the supernatural Christian salvation first disclosed in Christ and his church. In our day, this is the standpoint chiefly adopted by the Roman Catholic Church.

J. Braun places heavy emphasis on the exclusively preparatory character of the OT and on its being done away with by the coming of Christ; cf. *Handbuch der katholischen Dogmatik*, *s.v.* "Altes

Testament"; "Reich Gottes"; "Testament." My formulation here is based on oral discussions with Roman Catholic theologians.

(7) The standpoint that interprets the Old Testament typologically as proclamation of Christ. We shall be discussing this view in detail, since it is championed in some circles today with particular intensity.

(8) The standpoint that interprets the Old Testament allegorically. The Old Testament itself is an allegory, not so much of the historical Jesus as of the eternal Christ, that is, of the eternal salvation that in some way is granted to us in connection with the Christian church.

(9) The standpoint that sees the Old Testament as fulfilled in Christ in the sense that it comes into force for all nations and so achieves direct and full validity in the worship and life of a people. Thus the Sabbath is kept on Saturday, the father seeks a wife for his son, circumcision is practiced. This might be called the view of sectarian impatience.

It may be relevant to recall that in the sixteenth century the dominant link between rationalism and spiritualism could lead in related circles to the radical rejection of the OT on the one hand and its one-sided glorification on the other. Anabaptism took a very OT course in Münster, where it had the sense of being the true Israel. Rothmann declared there: "The true sum of all divine truth and will is to be found in the five books of Moses, by which conduct is to be directed." Even circumcision was practiced. Much later still, in 1614 and 1615, some Baptists went over to Judaism; cf. W. J. Kühler, *Geschiedenis der Nederlandsche Doopsgezinden*, pp. 82, 111, 118, 146, 461. The Reformed church in Holland was also faced by conversions to Judaism at that time; cf. H. H. Kuyper, *De Post-acta van de synode van Dordrecht*, pp. 268, 281, 441.

(10) The standpoint that interprets the Old Testament in terms of salvation history, that is, as a phase or series of phases on the ascending or descending line of the progressive march of revelation to clarity and fulness. In general, this is the Reformed attempt at a solution. Salvation history and the external history of Israel are identified, or at least very closely related. Cocceius, with his slight disparagement of the Old

Testament situation as one in which the saving benefits of the New Testament are not yet possessed in reality, can be fitted into the Reformed view.[13] Baumgärtel firmly rejects this, seeking instead an understanding in which the Old Testament is relevant for personal faith.[14]

A forest of questions is posed by all of this. We shall seek a path through that forest by limiting ourselves to a discussion of three points: (1) the Old Testament as such and its exegesis; (2) does the Old Testament already see Christ? and (3) the necessity of the Old Testament for the Christian church.

Footnotes to the Introduction

[1] Goppelt, *Typos,* p. 4.

[2] For the first centuries, cf. Koole, *De overname van het OT door de christelijke kerk* and Klevinghaus, *Die theologische Stellung der apostolischen Väter zur AT Offenbarung.* Klevinghaus somewhat uncritically measures the positions of the post-apostolic fathers by the Lutheran solution. A fine account carrying the history further is Diestel, *Geschichte des AT in der christlichen Kirche,* although one would have liked more on the theological background and context.

[3] It is well, I think, to recognize a difference in perspective between "church of God" and "church of Jesus Christ," even when they denote the same entity.

[4] On the terms "apostolate" and "Christianization," see my article "Theologie des Apostolates."

[5] Cf. the four methods worked out by Baumgärtel: (1) quotation to express one's own thoughts; (2) proof from prophecy; (3) typology for us; (4) allegory; *Verheissung,* pp. 72-86.

[6] Schleiermacher, *Der christliche Glaube,* sections 12, 132.

[7] Hirsch, *Das AT und die Predigt des Evangeliums.* Baumgärtel seeks to differentiate his own view from that of Hirsch; *Verheissung,* p. 148.

[8] *Institutes* II.xi.1.

[9] Cf. Bultmann, "Weissagung und Erfüllung."

[10] Baumgärtel, *Verheissung,* p. 92.

[11] This is the line that runs from Clement of Alexandria to Heiler; cf. Korff, *Het christelijk geloof en de niet-christelijke godsdiensten,* pp. 109f. The same view may be seen in Schleiermacher, *Der christliche Glaube,* sec. 12.

[12] Cf. on this my essay "Theologie des Apostolates," pp. 11-14.

[13] Baumgärtel, *Verheissung,* pp. 145, 111.

[14] Cf. Van Genderen, *Herman Witsius,* p. 163. This position has found a recent advocate in P. J. Roscam Abbing, *Diakonia,* and "De kerk en het OT."

CHAPTER ONE

THE OLD TESTAMENT AS SUCH
AND ITS EXEGESIS

It may seem that our main concern ought to be with the question, Does the Old Testament deal with Jesus Christ and can it be a source for the church's preaching of Christ? I think it will become clear as we proceed that this only seems to be the main problem we have to deal with. At any rate, we shall postpone this question for the moment in order to consider several preliminary questions.

I

The first question is whether the Old Testament is dealing with the same God as the New Testament, or — to reverse the order — whether the New Testament is dealing with the same God as the Old Testament.

I am thinking of Calvin's emphasis in his commentary on Hebrews 1:1. He seeks the unity of the OT and NT very definitely in God, not in Christ: "he sets before us one God . . . because God, who is always like Himself, and whose Word is unchanging, and whose truth is unshakeable, spoke in both together." Remember that it is at all points a distinctive characteristic of Reformed theology, both in thought and life, to work back through Christ to God.

Here is a question of fundamental importance for our subject. If the answer is no, the Christian church cannot and should not have anything more to do with the Old Testament. If the answer is yes — the God of the Old Testament *is* the same as the God of the New — we must not be misled by the remarkable dualities of the religion of Israel and the religion of the gospel of Jesus Christ and of the literature of Israel and the literature of primitive Christianity. These are real dualities; nonetheless, both circle around the same pole. How are we to understand this?

Eichrodt tries to understand it by laying stress on God, as Calvin does, and by adding a note on the establishment of the kingdom on earth. "For in encounter with the Christ of the gospels there is the assertion of a mighty living reality as inseparably bound up with the Old Testament past as pointing forward into the future. That which binds together indivisibly the two realms of the Old and New Testaments — different in externals though they may be — is the irruption of the Kingship of God into this world and its establishment here. This is the unitive fact because it rests on the action of one and the same God in each case; that God who in promise and performance, in Gospel and Law, pursues one and the self-same great purpose, the building of His Kingdom."[1]

The noteworthy thing about this question of ours is that it is a question of scholarship and of faith. On the basis of faith, it will be answered yes or no — by the Jew as well as by the Christian. In the scientific study of the Old and New Testament materials we must, and in fact do, adopt one or the other view. H. Bornkamm, for example, states that "a theological concept of the Old Testament . . . presupposes that the God who speaks and acts in the Old Testament is God himself, the Father of Jesus Christ."[2]

But this is not the end of the matter. At the same time, it is a constant concern of scholarship to take up this question and seek the answer to it, to investigate the phenomenological structure of the words, the connections of meaning and thought, the historical events, the whole content of what happens and what is said in the Old Testament and the New. To do that is constantly to be dealing with men in their relation to their God and consequently with God in his relation to these men. It all boils down to the question, Is he the same God? Is there a genuine interrelationship between the Old Testament and the New? The question is significant, not only ecclesiastically, but also from the standpoint of religious and world history. Unfortunately, Old Testament scholars in general fail to see this question as an important part of their study. Either they presuppose the identity of the God of the Old Testament with the God of the New Testament at once as a starting point, or they show hardly any interest in the matter at all.

Note that this is not the same as asking whether the one with whom we have to do in the Old and New Testaments is really God. If the God of the New Testament is the same as the God of the Old, then the Old Testament God in his distinctiveness must be taken up into this identity. He has his own name. He is also undoubtedly a national God. When Luther translated the Old Testament he used "God" or "Lord" to render "Yahweh," as the Septuagint and the Vulgate had done.[3] But in the light of historico-critical study this is no longer possible. And one cannot escape the problem by looking at the Old Testament through the eyes of the New and seeing "the guiding hand of God in the history of Israel's complicated struggle as it searched for clarity."[4] On the basis of the New Testament one cannot speak of God like that. In the New Testament God is the Father of our Lord Jesus Christ. This is a much more stringent peculiarity than the fact that God is called — and is — *Yahweh* in the Old Testament. Hence it is most important for both faith and systematic theology that God be left his Old Testament name and that it then be asked whether we have to do with the same God in the Old Testament as in the New. Only then can the sharp contours of the question be seen. And then we can no longer render it innocuous by saying with a nebulous certainty that of course it is "God."

The fortuitous situation exists in Holland that Bible translations since the seventeenth century have used the form *"Here"* for "Lord" (rather than *"Heer"*), thus giving the word something of the feel of a proper name, which means that it can serve quite well as a rendering of "Yahweh." E. Brunner takes a different view altogether. He feels that "Yahweh" should be dropped as a proper name (*Dogmatik,* I, 124, 142; Eng. tr., 119, 138) and believes that he can show that it loses the significance of a proper name even in the OT itself.

If one respects the distinctiveness of the biblical God in this way (annoying though it may be in philosophical reflection), a further, very different question arises. Is this God the same as that of paganism or a different God? The Old Testament says that Yahweh has chosen the people of Israel, that in so doing he is only the God of Israel, and that he is the God of one people in such a way as to appear to be a national God. Yet the Old Testament also says that other nations too are men who came from him (Ps. 9:20). He has not left himself without a witness among them. From the very beginning he has had dealings among them and with them. To that degree we find the same God in the Bible as in paganism. But he is no self-evident and perspicuous God. And under no circumstances can or should we begin with the general — the pagan or philosophical concept of God — and then try to find it in the particular — the reality of God — to use Eichrodt's phrase[5] — in Israel and in Jesus Christ. For between the general and the particular lies the fact of the choice of Israel and, along with that, the reality of God's special revelation in this world.

II

This naturally gives rise to a second question. How are we to handle the Old Testament, not just religiously and in faith, but also scientifically? To put it more plainly, Does revelation lie *behind* or *in* the texts, the parts, and the totality of the Old Testament? Can one establish that revelation took place in Israel by the methods of scholarship? In this connection we should note that the attitude of a neutral scholarship, which takes no account of revelation, is just as much a presupposition as any other, as W. J. de Wilde points out.[6]

For the moment, we shall leave aside as subsidiary any questions about revelation in the New Testament, such as who Jesus Christ is and in what scientifically or philosophically responsible sense one can speak of revelation in a systematic context. The question that concerns us is, Can we apprehend scientifically an historical revelation to Israel?

The historical approach to religion has taught us to relate the distinctive Old Testament understanding to the world around it, and yet also to consider the unique configuration that results from Yahweh's having worked on the elements of mythical and magical conceptions of the ancient Oriental and pagan world as a magnet works on iron fragments. The phenomenological approach to religion refers us to the intentional structure of the language, thought, and experience of the Old Testament. From the standpoint of systematic theology one may refer to the unparalleled destiny of the people of Israel in history. On these presuppositions, one may then seek the message of this book for the world today, even if only by means of existential interpretation, by the confrontation of the self-understanding of the Old Testament with that of modern man.

Discussing the historical approach to the OT, E. Sellin maintains that this method, "which set in during the second half of the previous century, continued to prove increasingly the religious superiority of the Old Testament over all other religious literature of the ancient Orient"; *Die Religion in Geschichte und Gegenwart*, I[2], 984. I prefer not to speak of superiority. Paganism, even including its magic, is profound and beautiful. From a human standpoint the idealism implied in paganism is to be rated more highly than the message of the Bible, even that of the NT. One should speak of the distinctiveness and uniqueness, not the superiority, of the Bible compared with paganism.

But can one really break through to revelation by means of scholarship? Or does one have to ascribe everything here to faith and unbelief? The latter, I believe, is undoubtedly the case. The ultimate and decisive things of life take place not in the sphere of reason and understanding but in the sphere of the heart and conscience. Why the message of the Old Testament instead of the message of the clay tablets, the Gilgamesh Epic, the Book of the Dead, or the dialogues of Plato? The decision is one of faith or unbelief.

But it is not a purely arbitrary decision. Authority here is supported by authority, since the Christian church cannot believe in Jesus Christ without taking the Old Testament along with him. For Jesus finds God and himself in the Old Testament.[7] Furthermore, faith does not find revelation in the Old Testament in the form of something magical that effects salvation, but in the form of a message whose content can be ascertained by scholarship. Above all, theological scholarship can show phenomenologically that the structure of the biblical understanding of being is radically different from that of the nonbiblical understanding. Man has to choose here: he is forced to live either nonbiblically or biblically, receiving salvation and listening to revelation.[8]

One is surely moving in the direction of a magical view of the Bible if he says with Valeton that the texts as we have them are often fallible (we no longer have the autographs), but that God can speak to us through the errors too; that the question as to what makes the Bible God's Word arises on a different level from that of scholarship; and that questions of introduction are of no significance for faith; *Het OT en de "critiek,"* pp. 11, 20f.

This raises a pertinent question. Does it affect scientific exegesis to hear God's message in the Old Testament and recognize it as revelation? Can scholarship investigate only the human echo of revelation or — even less — only what men comprehend as revelation? Can it treat this as purely human? Or can one reach the revelation of God through the texts, so that the exegesis of the Old Testament is a department of theological scholarship? Even more, can one encounter and hear God in the actual texts? Must we agree with H. W. Wolff that "if the expositor stands without a key before the door of God's Word, only one anxiety will fill him, that he is really knocking at the door, which is the text, and that he really hears the voice that comes to him through this door"?[9]

This is the nerve of the problem of Scripture. Is Scripture only a record of revelation, the human account of a divine event that stands behind it? The concept of a "witness to revelation" carries us an important step forward. But is not the writing also to be regarded as an element in revelation? Does not God's Word also become Scripture, a book? To be sure, this is not the only thing it becomes: it becomes history; it even becomes flesh. But does it not also become a book, Scripture? If so, is not the Bible more than a record of revelation or witness to it? Is it not a means of revelation?

T. C. Vriezen says, in *Hoofdlijnen der theologie van het OT*, p. 72, that "Scripture is God's Word in the transferred sense of the human rendering, that is, record, which embraces the words of God given in Israel by the prophets, but Christ is God's Word as the personal will of God expressed in the world among men. He is in a direct sense the incarnate Word; Scripture, however, is God's Word in an indirect sense." This type of dogmatics not only handles terms and concepts in a hazy and volatile manner but also makes light of the place that the written Word has in revelation according to the Christian faith. Holy Scripture is a special form of divine revelation, not just a record of the act of revelation. On this see E. Brunner, *Offenbarung und Vernunft*, pp. 153f.; Eng. tr., pp. 134f.

In relation to questions like these one is forced to take the concept of inspiration in a broad sense. The inspiration of Scripture is not identical to revelation, which took place *then,* in history. Nor is it merely the inspiration of the authors of the Bible, but the inspiration of Scripture. Hence the concept tells us not just how Scripture came into being *then,* but also how it is to be heard and to be read *now.* Inspiration is in the present tense as well as the perfect. In relation to the historical core of the Christian faith, which finds salvation in an event in history, we can never escape these many-sided questions in our theological studies. In Christianity the book plays a role, though it is not the one and only thing that counts.

One is reminded of the saying of J. A. Bengel in *Gnomon: "Divinitus inspirata est, non solum dum scripta est, Deo spirante per scriptores; sed etiam, dum legitur, Deo spirante per scripturam, et scriptura ipsum spirante."*
If one limits inspiration to the authors, one must reckon with the consequence that it is no longer possible to maintain the distinction between the prophets and apostles in their office and all the other children of God in their consciences; and one is forced to view inspiration as a miraculous supernatural event in the past. The idea of "graphic" inspiration (Scripture itself inspired) is the very thing to protect us against supernaturalism. It expresses dogmatically the objective fact that, phenomenologically, the Bible is characteristically different from paganism.

Thus the question whether one can encounter and hear God in the actual texts is an urgent one. In this connection the exegesis of Martin Buber is a remarkable portent for all the scientific exegesis that has been pursued in Protestant Christianity during the last centuries.[10] With almost legendary philological knowledge and human sympathy Buber has been able to make the texts alive from within. On the bosom of the Old Testament he has drunk the living words of God. We may be suspicious of some of the more violent constructions and hypotheses of his exegetical work and we may object to some of them, but we cannot help acknowledging that in his work specialized exegesis is practiced under faith's hypothesis of recognition of revelation.

What does that mean? On the one hand, it means that there is an exclusive desire for exegesis alone, exegesis "without epithet," the kind of exegesis that is not an expert and more or less mysterious art. On the other hand, it means commitment to an exegesis without limits, for this is an exegesis that goes to the heart of what is at issue in the words. One cannot, I think, easily exaggerate the difficulty of the hermeneutical problem as such or of general hermeneutical method. This is true not only of biblical exegesis. On the one side stands the exegete, pursuing his task, bringing himself along as a living being together with the whole world around him. Although he works philologically, his work is always within a specific sociological context. At this point one can hardly be too critical in scholarship. Truly scholarly and critical work can be done only when one keeps constantly in view the active subject in all its breadth and depth. On the other side, however, stands   the object of exegesis — the author, with the matter that engaged his attention. That man, whether foolish or wise, in faith or unbelief, in election or reprobation, is concerned with God. This applies to all literature, to all men. For a man can be understood only in and by his relation to God and God's relation to him.

This depth and difficulty of the hermeneutical problem is also true of the exegesis of the Old Testament. But if — within the framework of the Christian church or Christianized culture — we cut through this knot with a decision of faith and thus proceed on the assumption that revelation has taken place in the Old Testament and is to be sought there, we certainly cannot be content with theological scholarship until we have somehow won through to this revelation in the exegetical sphere.

W. Zimmerli and A. H. Edelkoort have noted that the weapons with which the OT has been contested in the last few centuries were forged in the smithy of Protestant theology, and have pointed out, correctly, that this consideration is a summons to reflection and humility. Cf. Edelkoort, "De motieven van den strijd tegen het Jodendom," p. 104. Buber's exegesis recalls an old Reformation principle that goes back to Jerome: truth does not stand *formaliter* in Scripture, but has to be grasped *ex contentis; ne putemus in verbis Scripturarum esse Evangelium, sed in sensu; non in superficie, sed in medulla; non in sermonum filiis, sed in radice rationis.* Cf. H. J. Honders, *Andreas Rivetus*, pp. 6f.

M. Noth, "Die Vergegenwärtigung des AT," pp. 9f., argues that "in reality there can be only one exegesis, whose work is controlled by its theme. This exegesis that is consonant with the matter may be more or less adequate or inadequate — and always inadequate as a work of man — but there can be no choice between different exegeses." A. R. Hulst's statement that exegesis not only cannot have an epithet but also knows no method, because it is possible only in faith and in the light of Christ, and that this means the end of method, makes the outlook bleak for exegesis as a branch of theological scholarship; *Hoe moeten wij het OT uitleggen?*, p. 126. In his *Dogmatik*, I, 45, C. Stange maintains that NT work done from the point of view that revelation is sought and found in the texts "will be theological in the special sense and will lead to such results as the philologist can achieve." In the last resort this thought has never been clear to me.

Baumgärtel brings out well the difficulty of the hermeneutical problem; "Ohne Schlüssel vor der Tür des Wortes Gottes?", pp. 419f. He is not very clear, however, on the relation between the work of the theologian and that of the philologist. In my view, one can solve this problem — and consequently the question of the distinctiveness of theological scholarship and the theological faculty — only if one realizes that method theology does not have to do anything different from what other sciences might do, but it has to set an example for all sciences by understanding the words in terms of the theme, and man and the world in terms of God, which it can do because it is acquainted with revelation and therefore with truth. This observation presupposes, however, that theology, scholarship, and the university are seen in the context of the *corpus christianum*. The theocratic concept is a necessary presupposition for theology as a science.

In the matter of the relation between exegesis and revelation, the limit is reached if one adopts Luther's starting point — that the biblical texts must be translated and expounded in the light of the whole Bible, and that one should not be afraid to give a distinctive turn to the philological meaning of words (cf. Bornkamm, *Luther und das AT,* pp. 209, 185-208; Eng. tr., pp. 247, 219-46) or if one states with Luther that the main concern is not to have a pure OT text but to see Christ, and that without him the pure text is useless, but with him the defective text can do no harm (cf. J. Koopmans, *Het oudkerkelijke dogma in de Reformatie,* p. 110). The value of this idea is its awareness that revelation is to be received only in the form of conscience — *knowing-with* God — but this insight is pushed to such an extreme that faith becomes a *knowing-with* God of what ought to have stood in the written Word, or at least of what God really would have sought to say. If one concentrates on Christ in understanding the Scripture, as Luther did, he can more easily affirm such an idea than if he thinks in terms of the kingdom of God, as I do. Moreover, in the relation of revelation and faith, one can never wholly eliminate the different authorities. Hence textual criticism and philology have a theoretical significance that nothing can destroy.

III

A disturbing third question is now inevitable. What is to be understood by revelation in the sense of the Old Testament itself? Whether we proceed exegetically in the sense of scholarship or in the strict sense of Christian theology, which recognizes the canonical authority of the Old Testament, we cannot approach the Old Testament with a specific concept of revelation and then forcefully try to rediscover that concept in the Old Testament.

One thing is surely clear. Revelation in the Old Testament sense cannot be understood merely as the impartation of teaching. This concept, with which many try to save themselves in the interpretation of revelation in Christ, is plainly inadequate. The Old Testament is too crude and too realistic for that. To be able to understand what revelation is there, one must resort to such expressions as the self-impartation or at least the presence of God among his people in a series of acts, a series that forms an ongoing history illumined by the continually new word of promise. T. C. Vriezen is — I think rightly — suspicious of applying the basic ideas of a theology of the Word to the Old Testament. The reference is to more than word; it is to the fellowship of the holy God with his chosen people (which forms the central concept in Vriezen's Old Testament theology).

J. Klevinghaus points out that already in the *Epistle of Barnabas* no interest is shown in Old Testament history, but only in the Old Testament as a book.[11] This alone is revelation. Korff speaks, distinctively enough, of a *preliminary* or *preparatory* coming of God in the old covenant, although he would have this construed as an actual coming, not just as preparation for coming.[12] Brunner refers to the Old Testament as a revelation that is provisional and serves as a precursor. In *Offenbarung und Vernunft* Brunner speaks in particular of a preparatory, provisional, nondefinitive revelation, though he once refers to it as pointing forward.[13]

In any case, the dimension of history is of predominant significance for what the Old Testament understands by revelation. I believe that in emphasizing this historical factuality one may go so far as to say that the category of religion is almost completely absent. With what is the Old Testament concerned? With concrete, secular things — possession of the land, the gift of posterity, the increase of the people, an eternal monarchy, a society based on righteousness and love. Not only the Israelites, but also the Old Testament authors and God himself, in his presence in the prophetic word and in the people of Israel, never get beyond these things. G. von Rad even asks whether the men of Israel could be aware that it was God who acted towards them historically in this way, in self-revelation.[14] He simply sees what happened in the Old Testament as having happened in all factuality; that is, he sees it in terms of "predestination."

The term *praedestinatio* is a dogmatic category with the help of which I would round out Von Rad's important view. The doctrine of predestination is the dogma used to describe God as the living and active God, whose activity transcends the possibilities of human awareness.

This means that even in the application of the Old Testament, and especially in exegesis, one cannot fall back on the piety or theology of the Old Testament. To be sure, piety and theology are found in the Old Testament. The men of the Old Testament definitely live in the grasp of God's hand. Specific lines of teaching run through the prophetic witness of the Old Testament. (Naturally this prophetic witness embraces the whole of the Old Testament, not just the "prophetic" books.) It is a task of biblical theology to try to draw these together in one or more unities. But one cannot grasp the quintessence in this way — an insight we reach very easily if we take seriously the thesis that Old Testament and biblical knowing rests on reality and is itself a form of historical reality. For the quintessence is God himself, the active, historical presence of God in Israel, so that it can be said to the people of Israel, "God is in you" (Isa. 45:14). The miracle of the real (as distinct from the spiritual) indwelling and gracious presence of God, Von Rad says, is the special thing vouchsafed to Israel.[15]

In the Christian tradition (including the Protestant) the recognition that the men of the OT lived in the grasp of God's hand has caused too great an importance to be attached to the Psalter. For Luther this was *the* book of the Bible; Bornkamm, *op. cit.*, pp. 7f.; Eng. tr., pp. 9f. In the Reformed tradition as well, the Book of Psalms was the center of the OT; Honders, *op. cit.*, pp. 69f.

It must be conceded to F. Baumgärtel that the history of piety is not the history of ideas, and that there will be no rationalistic or idealistic self-elevation above the realities of history in one's OT theology if he builds on the piety of the men of the OT; cf. "Der Dissensus im Verständnis des AT," p. 308. Nevertheless, it may be asked whether the history of piety is not just one segment of history, and whether it is in keeping with the OT to regard inner guidance as the most important factor in the light of the gospel, and then to single it out from the OT as a whole in terms of the external guidance of Israel; Baumgärtel, *Verheissung,* p. 123. The OT certainly does not understand itself in this way.

There is an important emphasis in G. von Rad, "Typologische Auslegung des AT," p. 28. Von Rad's stress is not merely that theological reflection is secondary in the OT — by comparison with the real history that the people of Israel lives out with God and with the witness it bears to this history in the OT — but also that theological reflection displays an unheard-of variability and fluidity and constantly produces fresh interpretation in a process that there is no desire to end. Every OT theology — for example, those of Eichrodt and Vriezen — confirms this insight. One can refer Hebrews 1:1 ("at many times and in many ways") to the various theological conceptions in the various sources; cf. Hulst, *op. cit.*, p. 59.

We cannot get by with the idea of progressive and increasingly brighter revelation. It is not just a matter of what men know about God — which may well be less clear and complete in the Old Testament than in the New. It is a matter of what God does among men. But can one say that that revelation is less *real* in one case than in the other? Can one make any use at all in this connection of the pet idea — often taken to be axiomatic in theology[16] — that only the person of Christ is completely transparent, so that revelation is "supreme" in him? This seems to me to be a highly uncritical theological procedure, not merely because it overlooks the fact that revelation is more concerned with what God does than with what man knows about him, but also because it disregards the fact that God is seen least of all in Jesus Christ. To know that God is present and active in Jesus Christ, no less is needed than the resurrection, the gift of the Holy Spirit, and the apostolate. The most we can say is that revelation progresses in terms of salvation history. For in this progress the reference is to connections and interrelations in the reality of history.

Calvin in particular sought to deal theologically with the OT along the lines of the idea of progressive revelation. "The covenant made with all the patriarchs is so much like ours in substance and reality that the two are actually one and the same. Yet they differ in the mode of dispensation" (*Inst.* II.x.2). "His appearance had before been indistinct and shadowed" (II.ix.1). "They were shadows at a time when Christ was still, in a manner, absent" (*Comm.* on Col. 2:17). "They only glimpsed from afar and in shadowy outline what we see today in full daylight" (II.vii.16). ". . . still far off and as if veiled. . ." (*ibid.*). "The image . . . which before had been begun in indistinct outline only" (*ibid.*). In the NT, grace "is put before our very eyes. They [the prophets] had but a slight taste of it; we can more richly enjoy it" (II.ix.1). The Old Testament is *literalis* because it still has an earthly flavor, while the New Testament is *spiritualis* (*Corpus Reformatorum,* LXVII, 318). In itself, then, the OT is weak and imperfect, whereas the NT is eternal and never changes. In the

NT Christ appears to us in full glory with no veil between (II.ix.1). A monograph on Calvin and the OT would be most useful.

It is important to note that if revelation is the revelation, self-impartation, or presence of God, it is the revelation of the God who acts and speaks. Hence, it is integrally interwoven with other words in the process of history, and the real concrete and earthly things with which it is concerned belong essentially to revelation. One cannot think of God apart from the world, especially in his revelation. Hence the history of the people of Israel is not just the sphere in which revelation takes place, so that God's Word may be heard only "in, with, and under" the content of the OT; H. W. Obbink, *Theologische bezinning op het OT*, pp. 16f.

At this point we must also ask to what end God is present in Israel and has dealings with it. Is it solely or supremely for the redemption of man? Can one view the Old Testament in so one-sidedly soteriological a light? Does not redemption take place rather for the establishment of the kingdom of God?

Here is a basic error, I think, in Baumgärtel's theological estimate of the OT. He says: "A theological statement can be only an evangelical statement, that is, an assertion on the basis of the gospel"; "Der Dissensus," p. 299. Also: "There should be no doubt as to the goal, which is also the starting-point, of the hermeneutical procedure, namely, that the theological apprehension of the Old Testament must be apprehension on the basis of faith, that is, of faith in Christ crucified and risen, and that all the work of biblical scholarship must be oriented to this and pursued in these terms. Because I do not think that this thesis can be disputed by theologians, I simply presuppose it as self-evident"; *Verheissung*, p. 144. Hence, it follows that "theologically speaking, if we are to grasp and present the content of the OT, only the promise in Christ can be made the hermeneutical principle" (*ibid.*, p. 102). "Only when we are able to understand the Old Testament word as witness to the promise in Christ can we speak of the theological relevance of the Old Testament" (p. 105). This is how the primitive church handled the OT and is the way the church's proclamation and OT scholarship must adopt (p. 159). It may be added that Baumgärtel adopts this attitude of the Christian church in assimilation to the experience of the individual Christian. "How far do I experience — under the gospel — this Old Testament word as mighty in me?" (p. 112). The OT word must be directly related to my personal faith (p. 111). Only then is it truly theological (p. 119). The basis of Baumgärtel's view of the OT is that under the promise of God, "we are truly associates of Israel; we stand with Israel under the promise, which has been put into effect for us along with Israel, and our own history is salvation history together with the (inner) history of Israel" (pp. 55f.), though it should be noted that the OT side of this salvation history is predominantly the history of disaster, the darkness of the natural man in his inward being, in the situation of unbelief (p. 84). The main point of my discussion is to show that the thesis Baumgärtel presupposes as an axiomatic starting point is wrong.

If we heed the fact that in the OT as well the setting up of God's kingdom is at issue, it will no longer appear to be so great a problem that the OT speaks so little of eternal life. As soon as one speaks exclusively or primarily in soteriological terms, this problem is seen in a wrong perspective.

Is the fall really so determinative a background in the Old Testament? The living God constantly builds on the fact that Israel and man are able and ready for that to which he calls them. The fall does not occupy so important a place *behind* the Old Testament history of revelation. It is *in* this history. It is a process of refusal and revolt. But one can hardly go so far as to say that in God's plan of salvation Israel is simply a mirror of the negative side, serving only to introduce sin and guilt and to bring them to light.[17] Israel and the Old Testament are at least to the same degree a mirror of the positive side. They reflect what the living God has in view for man and the world: his kingdom, his image, the law, theocracy.

Finally, we must look at how God is present and active in Israel. Already in God's relation to Israel there is an element of force. God forcibly sets forward his cause on earth. This forceful element comes much more strongly to the fore in Jesus Christ. The election of Abraham and Israel still respects man in his confrontation with God. The incarnation alters this, for now God is not simply God, but also man, in our place. Nevertheless, Abraham and Israel were at least called and elected apart from their own will and even directly against it. The way God deals with the Gentiles shows a much stronger respect for man and leaves him ultimate freedom.

Be that as it may, when we have to do with revelation in the Old Testament we have to do with concrete, historical and earthly facts. As Abraham Kuyper put it, our ideas are wrong if the national particularism of Israel does not fit into them.[18]

Baumgärtel can make little of this clinging to the material. For him national particularism and restriction to the world signify the limitation of the OT; *Verheissung,* pp. 19, 24, 26. They spoil the basic message of the prophets (p. 26). He thinks that we cannot grasp or explain these elements in the OT in terms of the promise in Jesus Christ (p. 63). In his view, the earthly element is not God's action but the view of OT religion concerning God's action. "The way of God is there presented to us as Old Testament religion saw it. No more"; "Der Dissensus im Verständnis des AT," p. 299. Von Rad rightly champions the materialism and thisworldliness and the offense of OT particularism, immanence, and salvation materialism; "Typologische Auslegung," p. 28; cf. his "Verheissung," p. 410.

IV

This leads to a fourth question. What is the relation between the exegetical and the homiletical in our wrestling with the Old Testament?

I put the question now while provisionally avoiding the problems raised by the specific preaching of Christ in the Old Testament. In order to get a clear view of questions relating to the Old Testament, we should first discuss the question apart from Christ. For the relation between the exegetical and the homiletical is already a problem — indeed a very pressing one — in terms of the Old Testament itself. One might formulate it as follows: if revelation takes place in the Old Testament, and if this revelation is the active historical presence of God in Israel, then the Old Testament chains us to the history that took place then, or at least to Israel.

A corresponding problem arises in relation to the saving event of Golgotha. This is difficult enough, though perhaps manageable. For this event is presented, *made present,* in the apostolic witness of the New Testament and in the official preaching and existence of the church, although there has been plenty of contention in the church as to the mode of this presentation. As Reformed churchmen we can at least say that we stand in the circle of salvation of which Golgotha is the center through the covenant, imputation, the sacrament, and at all events the Spirit.

But how are we related to Israel and its history? The Old Testament is concerned with specific events and situations there and then. It tells of these and of the presence of God in them. What can we do with such a book today? At the beginning of the previous century the older Liberals were led by their enlightened rationalism to the correct discovery that everything in the Bible is conditioned and limited in space and time.[19]

The older Liberals sought rational truths, but they found only or predominantly factual truths. Their demand for grammatical exegesis with its emphasis on the *e mente auctoris* also led them to the discovery that the authors wrote in a specific time and place. The great difference between the OT and the NT and the belief that the OT must be exegeted *e mente auctoris* played a significant role in this discovery. A man like P. Bosveld could declare quite radically that "Christ never spoke a word to us, only to his contemporaries." This thinking is further affected by the idea that in one's faith and systematic theology there is no real need for special revelation, since natural law suffices. The background has largely been abandoned in our time. But we are today very much concerned theologically with the discovery as such. We are constantly engaged in an intellectual working out of the Enlightenment.

How does God's voice come to us in the Bible? This is the homiletical question, which must be distinguished from the exegetical one. How do I hear in the texts the voice of God that spoke to men in that time and place? In systematic theology the homiletical question is just as important as the exegetical. Exegesis alone leads us nowhere. As H. W. Wolff says, "it is hard to exaggerate the difficulty of work undertaken in fulfilment of the hermeneutical task, though the question to be answered is basically clear and simple: What is the message that the text has for us in the name of God today if it still is to be the message of the Old Testament text, even though God has now uttered his definitive Word in Jesus Christ?"[20] Among other things he seeks the answer to the question of where the theme of the pericope is echoed in the New Testament.

Does God do anything among us today not only through but also with the Word that is thus conditioned and limited? Are *we* Israel, so that the divine events then took place as it were to us also? Or, in order to come to us, does it all have to go typologically by way of Jesus Christ, in whom Israel is concentrated? Or can we rescue ourselves with the more theological idea that while the *acts* of God belong to the past, the acts of *God* are always present, to use the concepts of a more or less mystical philosophy of history, as Martin Noth does: "These saving acts, which certainly came into the immediacy of history, and can be perceived by us only in this immediacy, are nevertheless always present as direct acts of God"?[21] And does this idea differ much from understanding biblical history as a kind of divine picture-book in which God's face is shown feature-by-feature — a kind of extended incarnation of the Word in which the historical aspect is rationalized through the medium of the divine picture?

It is important to recall at this juncture that revelation is not limited to the preached Word of Scripture. The word functions as revelation — even in preaching — only when the active presence of God is about it. Revelation is both by Word and also by Spirit, and the Spirit acts with the Word.

On this entire question, Von Rad remarks, "I belong to none of the twelve tribes; I do not sacrifice in Jerusalem; I do not hope for the transfiguration of the temple hill as in Isaiah 2:1-4; I am not even a proselyte. . . . The great display of God's saving provisions for Israel seems to pass me by because I do not belong to the historical people of Israel. And the Old Testament even to its final directions maintains the connection with this historical Israel"; "Typologische Auslegung," p. 31.

Oscar Cullmann says, "Inasmuch as the history of the people of Israel finds its fulfilment in the cross, it too affects my individual salvation"; *Christus und die Zeit,* p. 195; Eng. tr., p. 219. Baumgärtel points out very discerningly that what Von Rad says on this matter is ambiguous. On the one hand he views the Christian in direct relation to the content of the OT; on the other, he views him in a typological relation; "Der Dissensus," p. 303.

In any case we are urgently confronted here by the problem of the past and future in revelation, or, as one might also say, by the problem of Scripture and tradition. The notion of a river flowing down to the present is much easier for a man like Buber than it is for us. In this connection Buber speaks of the eternal reality.[22] He has in view the eternal Israel, which was then and is now; the eternal Israel in which God is — always different yet always the same in covenant faithfulness. In this eternal reality the spatially and temporally conditioned and limited Word can ring through and bring salvation. But we Gentile Christians cannot solve the problem so simply. For us the canon of Scripture has an inalienably Israelitish character. This is true of the Old Testament in particular, though it is true as well of the New Testament, for it too is the message of the Messiah. Thus the Word of God is more alien to us. Rome, understanding itself as eternal Rome, tends to overlook this; hence, it can see in tradition a stream in which Scripture or even Christ flows on. In so doing it has the happy knack of more or less forgetting the Old Testament. The Reformation, with its accent on the saving historical significance of the one sacrifice on Golgotha, has too strongly developed a sense of history, of Hebrew truth, to be able to negate the Israelitish character of the canon and the historical particularity of God's Word.

H. Diem, *Theologie als kirchliche Wissenschaft,* I, 81, quotes from a conversation between K. L. Schmidt and Buber, who describes his thoughts in a Jewish cemetery at Worms: "There beneath one does not have the tiniest shape; one has only stones and the ashes under the stones. One has the ashes, however scattered. One has the corporeality of men who have been. One has this. I have it. I have it not as corporeality in the space of this planet but as that of my own memory to the depths of history, to Sinai. I stood there and was linked with the ashes, and right through them to the patriarchs. This is the recollection of dealings with God which is given to all Jews. The perfection of the Christian place for God [Worms cathedral] cannot detach me from this. Nothing can detach me from Israel's age of God."

This accent of the Reformation churches means that they must take the problem of tradition much more seriously than the Roman Catholic Church can do. One might say that in its configuration it now becomes for the first time genuinely tradition. Salvation is "handed over" into the hands of the Gentiles. There is an element of betrayal here.[23] It is certainly a leap. To go to the heart of the matter, in the Reformation view of tradition not only is God (or Christ) taken seriously, but so, too, is man in his encounter with God. This encounter between God and man involves a leap in tradition. Salvation and truth are taken out of God's hands and put in the hands of men, who do all kinds of things with them, who even change their form, but who in any case give them shape in their own existence. Man has or comes to have *conscientia,* a conscience. He stands in the priesthood of all believers.

This is all much more applicable to the Old Testament in the Christian church than it is to the New. When we preach from the Old Testament, and when the full Old Testament witness to revelation is really passed on, this can take place only under the great presupposition that in the Spirit there is an incidental repetition of Israel — no matter how much it is all related to Jesus Christ and his work of salvation — which fulfils and establishes all things. Around Christ and by the Spirit we are appointed and made. For there is a *corpus christianum* as well as the *corpus Christi* (Rom. 9:24-29; 11:16-24). In addition to the church, we have the life and world that are to be sanctified and Christianized. There is also theocracy. This is perhaps the final prospect; in Israel it is, *a priori,* the first. Between Israel and the Christian people there lies not only tradition but also an antitypical relation. Things are seen as in a mirror, from the other side, in inverted order.

As I see it, one can preach the Old Testament in the Christian church only when one pays attention to this eschatological, theocratic perspective, so that Christian preaching is not merely a preaching of Christ, but also a preaching of the kingdom. Preaching will then be dealing with the concrete earthly things that are at issue in the Old Testament as well. The ordinary things of the world, seen spiritually, are the most important. In comparison, the New Testament seems at a first glance to be somewhat more spiritual. If the church's preaching is to be full preaching of the kingdom, in which all reality is set in the light of the Word and counsel of God, the Old Testament is quite indispensable. The New Testament is not enough. (One must even ask at times if Holy Scripture is adequate as a source of preaching in this full catholic sense.)

Whether OT exegesis and preaching are seen from the standpoint of tradition or of an antitypical relation, more than practical application *(accommodatio ad usum)* is at issue. Hulst also would go beyond the *e mente auctoris,* since the Holy Spirit uses the Word at different times, but he puts this under the head of practical application; *op. cit.,* pp. 118f., 123. It seems that Christian theology has not really mastered the category of history; perhaps the mystical realism of Buber would suit us better.

Hulst shows that exegesis is more than a mere link between the Bible and preaching. It is itself witness and proclamation, and this means that "it must somehow be related to the church's proclamation of Christ"; *ibid.,* pp. 123, 125. But here everything is too much compressed. The church's preaching is fully christologized; exegesis and homiletics are equated; the category of history with its "then and there" and "here and now" is not respected. A broader systematic theology is demanded if one is to master the questions at issue here.

Furthermore, it is only thus that there is a special place for the people of Israel in God's plan for the world. If we relate the Old Testament exclusively to Christ and find the people of Israel only in the body of Christ, we cannot integrate the Jews, the synagogue, and the State of Israel into our systematic theology. But if we respect more strongly the independence of the Old Testament, the free power of God in his dealings with Christian nations as incidental repetitions of Israel, and yet also the antitypical relation between the *corpus christianum* and the people of Israel, we shall see (1) that God is always concerned only about the earth; and (2) that it is possible at any time that he may return afresh to his people Israel; and that either way he will not be unfaithful to what he has done in his Messiah Jesus.

At any rate, in such contexts Old Testament Scripture can function with full weight and with its own canonical authority as a source of preaching in the church of Christ. This preaching is then, as preaching, more than gospel. It is the ministry of the Word.[24] It is thus also the preaching of the law, the kingdom, the image of God. In the apostolic course of the Word throughout the world, Old Testament preaching especially is on the offensive, though naturally there are within it many possibilities of synthesis with pagan life.

The NT can be assimilated more easily to pagan parallels, but when this happens, misunderstandings always result. The OT and its witness to God's salvation and right constantly summon the church and preaching back to special revelation, on the basis of which they may then seize and sanctify paganism.

Footnotes to Chapter One

[1] Eichrodt, *Theologie des AT,* I, 1; Eng. tr., I, 26.

[2] Bornkamm, *Luther und das AT,* p. 225; Eng. tr., p. 264.

[3] *Ibid.,* pp. 165f.; Eng. tr., pp. 195f.

[4] *Ibid.,* p. 226; Eng. tr., p. 265.

[5] Eichrodt says that the biblical revelation "proclaims, not a complete and closed body of teaching, but the reality of God becoming manifest in history"; *Theologie des AT,* I, 274.

[6] De Wilde, *Het probleem van het OT,* p. 19.

[7] Korff, *Christologie,* II, 15-21.

[8] Miskotte's *Edda en Thora* is an interesting attempt in this direction.

[9] Wolff, "Der grosse Jesreeltag," p. 79. It is plain that what is in view is hearing God; cf. p. 104.

[10] Kraus, "Gespräch mit Martin Buber," pp. 60-64.

[11] Klevinghaus, *Die theologische Stellung der apostolischen Väter,* pp. 38f.

[12] Korff, *Christologie,* II, 21ff.

[13] Brunner, *Offenbarung und Vernunft,* pp. 100ff., 151ff.; Eng. tr., pp. 81ff., 132ff.; cf. *Dogmatik,* I, 56; Eng. tr., I, 48.

[14] Von Rad, "Predigt über Ruth, I," pp. 1-6; "Typologische Auslegung," pp. 26ff.

[15] "Typologische Auslegung," p. 27.

[16] Cf. for example Rowley, *The Relevance of the Bible,* pp. 24ff.

[17] So Barth, *Kirchliche Dogmatik,* II/2, 215ff.; Eng. tr., II/2, 195ff.

[18] A. Kuyper, *Uit het Woord,* II, 1: "Dat de genade particulier is," p. 180.

[19] Cf. Sepp, *Proeve eener pragmatische geschiedenis der theologie,* pp. 3, 50, 60f., 243; Roessingh, "De moderne theologie in Nederland," p. 20; Fiolet, *Een kerk in onrust,* pp. 17f.

[20] Wolff, "Der grosse Jesreeltag," p. 97.

[21] Noth, "Die Vergegenwärtigung des AT," p. 16.

[22] Kraus, "Gespräch mit Martin Buber," pp. 60-64.

[23] Cf. Barth, *Kirchliche Dogmatik,* II/2, 535; Eng. tr., II/2, 482.

[24] I owe this distinction to P. J. Hoedemaker.

CHAPTER TWO

DOES THE OLD TESTAMENT ITSELF ALREADY SEE CHRIST?

It is surely evident from what we have said that historical revelation in the Old Testament and its presentation in Old Testament preaching are not only relevant to us by way of Jesus Christ and in terms of typology. But to say it this way is to leave unanswered the question of whether or not typology might be a valid way. Is the Old Testament, with its authority, only a basis for preaching the kingdom, or is it also a basis for preaching Christ? Can we wholly separate the one from the other? In the light of the New Testament it must certainly be said that the kingdom is grounded in the sacrifice of Jesus Christ and has found a firm place on earth only in him. On the one side, then, the "cross"-aspect of the kingdom of God permeates the whole preaching of the kingdom in the Christian church. On the other side, however, the preaching of the kingdom is concentrated in this "cross"-aspect. Or, like a dove, preaching folds the wings of the concept of the kingdom and perches on the cross. It proclaims Christ. But can it do this from the Old Testament perspective?[1] Is it legitimate — exegetically, not just homiletically — to use the Old Testament as a canonical source for preaching Christ? In other words, our question is not just "can we use the Old Testament in preaching Christ?" but "does the Old Testament itself already see Christ?"

I

My first observation on this question is that the whole of the Old Testament in its unity is not to be understood as one promise of Christ or even as issuing in one promise of Christ. Quite the contrary. The whole history of the people of Israel in the Old Testament is engaged in an ongoing movement from promise to fulfilment. Again and again the living God comes into the midst of his people with his Word, which breaks into the actuality of their lives, not only as prophecy, but also as promise, command, and threat. But already in the Old Testament there is fulfilment as well as promise. Promise sets Old Testament history in a movement towards fulfilment.

W. Zimmerli discusses promise and fulfilment in his essay "Verheissung und Erfüllung." He writes: "It should be clearly established that there is no prophetic promise that can be summed up in a single formula. . . . Prophecy closes with unsettling dissonance. *The* event of Yahweh, which should unite the themes of life and death proclaimed by the prophets [I think this is an illegitimate reduction of the prophetic expectations mentioned on pp. 45f.; A. A. v. R.] in a final fulfilment, has not come" (p. 46). Again: "In the Old Testament we hear no call that might bring this story to an end. On the contrary, we have to say that many promises are left in the air, many sayings contradict one another in direct content. Here the fulfilment of the anointed earthly monarchy is expected; here the fulfilment of the kingship of Yaweh that recognizes no earthly monarch. Here the radical replacement of Zion is intimated; here its final glorification at the end of the times is expected. One cannot work out a smoothly integrated sum of all promises in the Old Testament" (p. 52). "The whole history of the monarchy, according to the Deuteronomic view, takes shape as an honoring of the continually new prophetic word . . . even to the last detailed ramifications of the history of Israel" (pp. 40f.). Zimmerli also discusses the relation of the promises in the patriarchal stories to their fulfilment in the Exodus (pp. 34-38). "When we consider the whole of the Old Testament, we find ourselves set in a great history of movement from promise to fulfilment" (p. 51). Joshua 21:45 is an obvious testimony.

This movement towards fulfilment is not controlled by an unalterable plan. God allows free course to the history. Even before his words are fulfilled, and irrespective of whether they can later be fulfilled, they create a sphere of freedom in which there is room for repentance and conversion, for faith and obedience.[2] A way is made for all man's historical action in this freedom by the previously declared Word of God. That is, history has an inclination that stands under the clear word; thus, it is not the fulfilment of fate. It is continually perforated by the clarity and freedom given to man with the Word of God.

The whole structure of the relation between the living God and his elect demands a radical commitment to history. The promise is concrete and seeks concrete fulfilment, that is, fulfilment in earthly and visible things. This means also that the history is lived out as genuine history, that is, in the category of the future and with a constant awareness of the "not yet" or the "not yet perfectly," so that one is always in fact on the way somewhere. Past and present are also described in the light of the promise and are thus described hyperbolically.

Hence there is restless onward movement. The Old Testament is the book of the history of the people of Israel as this is dominated by promises, commands, threats, and prophecies. Typology — the linking of what follows to what precedes — is deep-seated in it, not only in relation to the Messiah, but also in the history as such. This is lived out typologically.

The clarity of history spoken of here is certainly not to be understood rationalistically. Rather, it is to be connected with the profound hiddenness of the divine meaning of this history, as Von Rad so strongly emphasizes; "Typologische Auslegung," p. 26. Zimmerli's reference to "a total history that overarches the generations and is controlled by a single will" ("Verheissung und Erfüllung," pp. 39f., 51) distinguishes the OT from the world around, in which the schema of prophecy and fulfilment does at least play a role (pp. 41f.). Luther also had a sharp eye for this historical reference and determination of God's promise in the OT; cf. Bornkamm, *Luther und das AT*, pp. 96-98; Eng. tr., pp. 112-14.

That neither present nor past but future is the category of historical thinking is the thesis of J. Huizinga, *De wetenschap der geschiedenis*, pp. 66, 95f.

"The whole of Old Testament history," Zimmerli writes, "insofar as it is history directed and imparted by God's Word, acquires the character of fulfilment — but in fulfilment the character of new promise" (*op. cit.*, pp. 40f., 51f.; cf. Von Rad, "Typologische Auslegung," p. 29.

On typology note Von Rad's remarks: "The 'tradition' shows zeal for God by already extending the events into types." One has to "speak of an eschatological element in these presentations. . . , inasmuch as they portray a definitive divine action as already actual in history." He also makes reference to the idea of a first and second exodus in the prophets. God will do something again similar to what he has already done; *ibid.*, pp. 29f.; cf. L. Goppelt, *Typos*, pp. 42-47.

What one can certainly say about Jesus Christ on this basis is that he is at least one act among others in this history of God with his people. This cannot be too greatly stressed. It is not good enough to point only to the prophetic, ethical knowledge of God that shines out in the form of the New Testament Christ and in which the brightest rays of the Old Testament find a common focus. If one falls back on this thought — understanding the Old Testament along the lines of presenting Christ in this sense — and thus selects certain parts from it, one is spiritualizing in earnest and forsaking the sphere of history. From the Old Testament standpoint Jesus Christ is either of theological significance only as an historical fact — as an act of God in the history with his people Israel — or he is of no significance at all. Whether the Old Testament already sees and evaluates this act of God is, of course, another question, which I can tackle more fully by making a second observation.

It is difficult to understand what T. C. Vriezen means when he calls Christ the message of God (*Hoofdlijnen der theologie van het OT,* p. 78) and says that he sheds further light as the focus of the rays of light in the OT (p. 70), and that he sums up (p. 70) and reveals the OT (p. 72). But Vriezen also uses such words as "to realize," "to become actuality," "actualization" (pp. 70, 72). At this decisive point in his book, his expositions are not distinguished by dogmatic clarity or precision.

In the cross as expiatory offering the active character of the person, coming, and work of Jesus Christ finds supreme concentration. The cross is an historical act in an even fuller sense than all the events of the OT. To see this is to settle the question of the relation between OT and NT in the doctrine of the atonement. If one asks how far and in what sense this act is Word (God has spoken through his Son and the Son is the Word), a difficulty arises. In any case one may not deduce from this a purely subjective doctrine of the atonement. For this act becomes Word to us only in the Spirit. The sacrifice of the cross as God's act sheds a wholly new light on the question of how the OT is fulfilled in Jesus Christ. The cultic elements in the OT will then have to be taken much more seriously than is possible in systematic theology, which is controlled by the prophetic ethical knowledge of God as the distinctive feature.

II

From the standpoint of the Old Testament — that is, in accordance with its description of the structure of Israel's history as history controlled and impelled by God's speaking — something new can undoubtedly take place, even in the sense of a radical turning. This new thing might take place so as to appear to be a new phase, an event that contains the seed of the future, of another new phase, so that it regards itself merely as one of many phases in God's dealings with his people. Or it might take place so as to appear to be the final phase, in which case all the problems in visible reality would be truly solved, for the final phase will be the eschatological fulfilment of God's ways of salvation,[3] and therewith the final consummation of history.

Here, it seems to me, is what makes our problem so difficult. How does the New Testament stand in this respect? It purports to be more than a mere prolongation of Old Testament history. As Zimmerli says, "Old Testament history is not simply extended without a break into that of the New Testament."[4] The New Testament knows of a new act so enormous, a new invasion and coming of God in history so gigantic, that it speaks of the *eschata,* the *eschaton,* and even the *eschatos* in the present; and carries this so far that it views Christ in various ways as the *telos* — in the sense of end or ending — of the law and the old covenant.[5]

The eschatological character of NT occurrence is not, I think, to be taken as meaning just that God now does his last deeds, so that now the things of the last time come on the scene. It also means that God himself comes. The whole eschatological thinking of the Bible is deeply rooted in the fact that the Bible knows God as the other confronting man.

But, rather remarkably, the New Testament gives no sign at all of depreciating the Old Testament. On the contrary, it refers to innumerable passages as fulfilments of the Old Testament, in which the Old Testament is genuinely honored and brought into full force for the first time.[6]

All the same, there is a most astonishing turn when the New Testament speaks of the *eschaton,* which has come in the present but is the center of time and history rather than the end. As a result, the Christian sense of time, in contrast to the Jewish and Old Testament view, lays the emphasis not on the past and future but on the center, the present perfect, Jesus Christ.[7]   (It is important to recognize that neither the Old Testament nor Judaism sees that time has a center as well as an end.)

Nevertheless, even in the New Testament the Christian life is dominated by promise and expectation. "We do not cease to pray for the coming of the kingdom and for deliverance from evil," Zimmerli notes, "nor do we set these things in the perfect."[8] As a result, the Christian life is on the way with the forefathers. As yet, only the shadows of the ultimate salvation are visible (Hebrews 11 and 12).

Wolff observes that "insofar as the church is a shadow of the future, the *umbrae* of the Old Testament are true of it too"; "Der grosse Jesreeltag," p. 103. This insight is of incalculable importance. The church has again been set in an OT situation, especially by the ascension. The shadows of the OT apply to it *quodam-modo* (Calvin), and thus the whole of the OT, particularly its social and political aspects, becomes significant again. Nor are we directed exclusively to the church (in Christ), but as the church of Jesus Christ we must be oriented to the world (in the *eschaton*). (I have developed these theses in greater detail in *De vervulling van de wet.*) The *méllonta* of Hebrews 10:1 cannot, then, be identified with their image, Christ. They are the eschatological light of the glory of God. Because that image stands before the glory of God, it casts shadows.

All this may be summed up in the remarkable appeal of the New Testament to the new covenant of Jeremiah (chapter 31) and Ezekiel (chapter 36), where God's law is said to be written on the hearts of men. It maintains that this new covenant is made, but finds it in the diametrical opposite of all inwardness, the sacrifice of Golgotha made at the very heart of history (Hebrews 8 and 10). At the same time the New Testament sees a duality of Messiah and Spirit. The Spirit fills history and the heart with the law of God, as the Spirit was also paradigmatically and vicariously in the heart of the Messiah (Ps. 40:8; cf. Heb. 10:5-10).

It is an oversimplification to limit oneself (with Zimmerli, "Verheissung und Erfüllung," p. 56) to saying that the NT fulfils the decisive contents of Jeremiah 31, but with the royal freedom with which a king "fulfils" a herald's call. Nor is the problem solved by saying simply (with W. J. de Wilde, *Het profetische getuigenis,* p. 117) that the new men whom God creates, according to Jeremiah, are to be found in Jesus Christ to the degree that it is said on the one hand: "This new *men* (but this is a singular, not a plural) is Jesus Christ," and on the other hand, "God has revealed in him the whole riches of his grace and wills to see the new people born from the new man Christ as a people without sin, because sin no longer exists in its thoughts." De Wilde also refers to the immediacy of knowledge of God in Christianity: "The decisive thing is not what is told you, but what God's spirit says to your hearts by the Word" (p. 120). This is a very different interpretation. It inclines towards the notion of an Inner Light and leaves no real place for official preaching as an essential mediation of salvation. A christological imputative fulfilment of the new covenant may certainly be deduced from the NT, but it is not found in Jeremiah 31.

Is the gospel of Jesus Christ and his Spirit a *new* phase or the *final* phase in God's dealings with his people Israel? We must answer this question before we can answer whether the Old Testament already sees Christ. But here a final turn is given to this whole set of problems; for the New Testament is obviously not meant to be merely a new phase, and yet it does not claim to be the last phase. Martin Buber and H. J. Schoeps can rightly declare that the world is not yet redeemed, but they are wrong, it seems to me, when they add that they cannot therefore believe that the Redeemer has already come.[9]

III

Properly to understand this remarkable integration of the New Testament into God's dealings with Israel, Christian theologians — and this is my third observation — draw our attention to the following points.

(1) It is already quite plain in the Old Testament that only Yahweh himself can legitimately interpret his promises, and he interprets them by the way he causes them to be fulfilled. Here, then, he remains free. This freedom of God is in marked contrast to man's freedom, which is created precisely by the promise. For things do not happen without words. They are publicly declared, so that man may know and act with God in repentance and conversion, faith and obedience. The whole cause of God seems to be dependent on man's conduct. But the problem of freedom lies deeper. The freedom of man seems to arise only when, understood as free will, it rests on the constant freedom of God, understood as free power. God remains free in the way he causes his promises to be fulfilled. Against this background one can try to understand Jesus Christ's person, coming, and work as the act of God, and consequently as God's fulfilment of his promises to Israel. Yet there is in this thought a remarkable reference to the primary author of Scripture, who here breaks through all the secondary authors. Historically and exegetically too, this applies not only to the relation of the New Testament to the Old, but also within the Old Testament. The true question is, how does God intend his promise? Do we really have to engage in retrospective exegesis?

On the freedom of Yahweh, see Zimmerli, "Verheissung und Erfüllung," pp. 47, 51f. F. Baumgärtel formulates the thought in its most radical form: God cannot be held committed to any one of the OT promises, which are only basic promises to Israel. In Christ he gives his true promise in full freedom, and this is to be distinguished in principle from a prophecy (*Verheissung*, pp. 28-36, 100f.).

H. J. Kraus ("Gespräch mit Martin Buber," pp. 72-74) engages in too one-sided a polemic against Buber's conception of man's power of decision. But Kraus does say that "comprehensive expositions would be needed to pursue and do justice to Buber in his final principles." There is here, it seems to me, an extremely important distinction between the OT and the NT. In the incarnation and the whole gospel of Jesus Christ, God forces through his cause on earth. This free power of God goes beyond the freedom of one who gives a promise to fulfil and interpret it. In this connection, it is noteworthy that Luther proves his doctrine of the bondage of the will and double predestination from the OT in particular (cf. Bornkamm, *Luther und das AT*, pp. 61ff.; Eng. tr., pp. 71ff.).

With respect to the matter of the primary and secondary authors of Scripture, Calvin (according to H. Schroten) sees the problem as follows: "A first fulfilment, directly envisaged by the prophetic biblical authors, takes place, as does a second fulfilment, just as directly envisaged by the Holy Spirit as the true author of Scripture"; *Christus, de middelaar*, p. 112. The second view is more perfect than the first. Naturally, the point of this understanding is not that the secondary authors are to be regarded as less important, but that the self-revealing God intends more (even in the words he inspires) than the authors of the Bible (can) grasp. One cannot evade this problem by trying to work through to revelation by way of exegesis; cf. Chapter One above. To emphasize the freedom of God in the fulfilment of his promises — a fulfilment that is then seen as the only legitimate interpretation of his promises — leads to difficulties. I think it is better not to try to establish the relation of the OT to the NT with the help of the distinction between the first and second authors of Holy Scripture, for this distinction introduces a docetic element into revelation — the recipient of revelation does not wholly understand what its giver says.

(2) The Old Testament cannot be reduced unequivocally to one promise. There are many promises, some of them contradictory. As a result, the Old Testament is fragmentary — a torso — not only in the sense that it still expects something, but also in the sense that it does not know exactly what it expects. In the Old Testament view of the future even the relation of the kingdom of Yahweh to the messianic kingdom is never very clear.[10] Hence a Christian theologian who assumes that God has cut this knot in Christ and given in him a plain fulfilment of all the contradictory promises is oversimplifying. Greater reserve is necessary here. To the very depths of Old Testament expectation, the people of Israel as a people, the land, posterity, and theocracy play a role that cannot possibly be eliminated. This role cannot be altered by regarding Christ and his church as the fulfilment, in other words, by spiritualizing. There is a surplus in the Old Testament, a remnant that cannot be fitted into the New Testament fulfilment.

The basic promises of the OT are, according to Zimmerli, (1) possession of the land; (2) posterity; (3) a worldwide history of blessing to counteract the worldwide history of the curse (Gen. 3—11 J); (4) I will be your God and ye shall be my people; "Verheissung und Erfüllung," pp. 36f. He also mentions (1) the Davidic promise; (2) the deliverer-king; (3) the branch; (4) the grace of David; (5) Zion; (6) the promise of the land and the presence of Yahweh; (7) the gathering of the dispersion; and (8) the resurrection of the people from the death of the Exile (pp. 45f.).

It is an oversimplification to identify the kingdom of God with the kingdom of the Messiah on the ground that the Messiah "can only be the visible embodiment of the kingdom of God, the manifestation of God in flesh and blood," as does A. H. Edelkoort, *Karaktertrekken der OT religie*, p. 22.

Similarly, Obbink argues that we need the NT in order to understand the OT in its true sense. Jesus Christ is the answer to OT expectation; and by and in this answer the expectation is no longer a torso but acquires end and meaning. Hence we must read the OT in the light of Jesus Christ; *Theologische bezinning op het OT*, p. 30.

May we distinguish between the one promise from God (the salvation found in his fellowship and kingdom) and the many forms of expectation that constitute man's reaction to the one promise, as does Obbink (*ibid.*, p. 29)? Baumgärtel goes furthest in this direction by making a radical distinction between human prophecy and divine promise. He says that the promise has "nothing in common with the earthly and national ties of the Old Testament," and that it is not a human word, by which faith could not live (*Verheissung*, pp. 32-35). Does this not lead to a docetic concept of revelation and go completely contrary to Luther? According to Luther, God and his speech have to become human if man is to make contact with them.

Can one really maintain with W. J. de Wilde (*Het profetische getuigenis*, p. 166) that Deutero-Isaiah is exclusively concerned with a spiritual dominion of Israel over the nations, that political aspects do not call for consideration, and that only the universal significance of the religion of Israel is at issue? De Wilde himself concedes (p. 167) that temporal and supratemporal statements continually accompany and permeate one another. Indeed, as long as one cannot be rid of Israel (the election), one cannot drop time, nor indeed the concrete realities of fulfilled time. The distinction between religious and political, or spiritual and secular, leads nowhere. G. von Rad is correct to emphasize very clearly that prophetic expectation in the OT is wholly fulfilled by the historical realities of the holy national life of Israel ("Typologische Auslegung," p. 24). The fulfilment of history, as OT prophecy realizes, involves the fulfilment of the history of God with his people.

The idea of a surplus or remnant in the OT that cannot be fitted into the NT fulfilment is rightly stressed by Baumgärtel: "To a large degree the prophecies of salvation (earthly, national expectations of the prophets, etc.) cannot be harmonized with the gospel at all"; *Verheissung*, p. 133. Whether this means that "too much" of the OT is theologically irrelevant, however, is definitely another question.

(3) The concern of the Old Testament expectation is prophetically with the coming personal Lord, God himself. "The coming event," Zimmerli says, "is the act of a personal God. The God who comes in person makes all the different expectations plain: Yahweh himself is the future of which they speak. . . . At its deepest base prophetic promise does not proclaim predictively a coming something, but him who comes, how he slays and how he also calls to life."[11] The subject, rather than the object, of the happening is decisive. To be sure, God acts in and with the people of Israel and the earth, but this is not the decisive thing. He himself is what really matters. Prophecies and predictions are to be regarded merely as something accidental. But then one can go a step further and say, "Well, then, he himself has in fact come in Jesus Christ."

But it seems to me that the following questions cannot be avoided: Is the object of God's action — all the circumference of his presence in Jesus Christ — really so unimportant? Do the world and God's action with it really stand so completely in the shadows behind the glory of the personal coming of God? Is there really no truth at all in the idea that God stands in correlation to Israel, that is, that he never wills to be alone and without his people Israel?[12] Is God's presence in Jesus Christ really the presence that occupies so central a place in the purpose of the Old Testament? In the Old Testament, is not God to come among his people as God, whereas in the New he has come as the God who is man?

Zimmerli writes that "as far as concrete contents and chronology are concerned, prophecy is governed by a surprising freedom and often by a very striking mutability"; "Verheissung und Erfüllung," p. 46. He also speaks of the "clearly recognizable relativity of the predictive element as compared with the promise of the approaching personal Lord" (p. 55). Inconceivably, Zimmerli thinks that he can defend himself in this way against Bultmann's theses, although Bultmann criticizes the OT precisely in terms of the approaching personal Lord.

Brunner comes to this conclusion: "Those four elements in the Old Testament revelation: the word, the act, the name, and the face, which, in the Old Testament, seem to point beyond themselves toward a hidden and as yet unrealized unity, have become a unity in Jesus Christ, and in so doing for the first time have received their full meaning"; *Offenbarung und Vernunft,* p. 126; Eng. tr., p. 109; cf. pp. 108-10; Eng. tr., pp. 91-93. The concept of the face of God in particular plays a significant role in this interpretation of the relation of OT and NT. Baumgärtel's thesis that the absolute principle "I will be your God" is the only thing in the OT relevant to us — from a NT standpoint — is along the same lines; *Verheissung,* pp. 26f., 105.

When Christian theologians discuss the centrality of God's presence in Jesus Christ to the purpose of the OT, they often run OT thoughts into one another. Thus W. J. de Wilde says: "This king, however, will be God himself, and he will exercise his dominion through his servant David" (in relation to Jer. 23:1-8; 33:14ff.; Ezek. 37:24-28); *Het profetische getuigenis,* pp. 147ff. According to Brunner, "This Shepherd is God himself, and yet — in the same chapter in Ezekiel — he is also 'My Servant David' who 'shall feed them, and be their shepherd' "; *Offenbarung und Vernunft,* p. 110; Eng. tr., p. 94. T. C. Vriezen rightly says: "Hence God's Messiah is the one who acts in God's name, but he is always secondary to God himself"; *Hoofdlijnen der theologie van het OT,* p. 180.

(4) In Old Testament expectation the reference is to the God who comes to slay and to make alive.[13] Christian theologians are often dazzled by this thought, by which they establish a direct relation to the center of the gospel, the crucifixion and resurrection. I should think one would be hesitant to go so far as to say that death and resurrection are integral to God and his coming. In the Old Testament death and resurrection are seen only indistinctly as that which will have to happen time and again in the mortal crisis of this age. This mortal crisis continually recurs, not just because of the inadequacy and obstinacy of man and nation but also (if I may put it thus) because of the contentious insistence of Yahweh, who is never satisfied until he has man's heart, his very self.[14] Hence the core of the problem between man and God seems constantly

to be: "Die and come to be." Kohlbrügge and Böhl, with more or less prophetic fixity of purpose, can find, in this light, the justification of the ungodly throughout the Old Testament, that is, the work and benefits of Christ rather than Christ himself.

In the New Testament, in Jesus Christ, death and resurrection certainly seem to be that around which everything revolves. But they are not the real point at issue, not even in the New Testament. He died and rose again that he might be Lord of the dead and the living (Rom. 14:9). To put it in Old Testament terms: what matters is everyone sitting under his vine and fig tree, in other words, earthly possessions and inhabiting the earth where righteousness dwells — all to God's praise. The element of the earth is not eliminated, not even when the cross of Jesus Christ is planted in that earth. Here too is a surplus in the Old Testament as compared with the New.

G. von Rad disputes those who argue "as if the 'historical' projections of prophetic predictions contained no reference whatever to salvation and judgment in Christ!"; "Verheissung," p. 410. Cullmann maintains that "it is only by reference to Jesus of Nazareth, who was crucified under Pontius Pilate, that the entire Old Testament can be interpreted as pointing to Jesus Christ. Only now can it be shown how sin and redemption, which constitute the theme of all the process [!], make necessary from the outset this particular process, which has as its goal an incarnate and crucified Christ, and which develops in a time process to the incarnation and crucifixion"; *Christus und die Zeit*, p. 120; Eng. tr., p. 136. Obbink speaks to the same effect: OT believers "have had faith in the same reality of the saving will of God as was made visible and perceptible in later centuries in the person of Jesus Christ"; *Theologische bezinning op het OT*, p. 22. The trouble with this understanding of the concept of saving will, however, is that even in the NT a discrepancy exists between the kingdom and the cross as elements in this will.

If we accept the idea that God's concern is to slay us so that he may make us alive again, a Gnostic element remains in our interpretation and proclamation of the gospel of Jesus Christ, as though the point of the cosmic process were to be found in the atonement, in the fact that we begin to live by forgiveness! Surely doxology is more than soteriology.

IV

This leads to my fourth observation. We cannot handle the

strange integration of the New Testament into God's dealings with his people Israel by trying to harmonize the Old Testament and the New along the lines suggested above. On the contrary, we must state plainly that at certain essential points the Old Testament and the New are not coextensive. This incongruence arises not just because each new act of God is to some extent incongruent with what precedes, but particularly because there are in the New Testament certain central matters of which no trace is found in Old Testament expectation. As more or less typical examples of this incongruity, consider the following:

(1) We are already surprised to find that the Old Testament sometimes holds out the prospect that God will himself come among his people, as God, not as man, as in the New Testament fulfilment. But we are surprised anew to note that the Old Testament sometimes holds out the prospect of a Messiah, a man who will come in God's name to do God's work on earth, but that then in the New Testament it is God himself who comes as the Messiah. (This point — that it is God himself — must be distinguished from the point that we are dealing with the same God in the New Testament as in the Old, about which we spoke in Chapter One.) But there is nothing about this in the Old Testament. Is there, in fact, in the New Testament? Or has dogma incorrectly understood and developed what is said there? In any case the Christian church is well advised, if it keeps to the basic lines of dogma, to see the incongruence at this point clearly. The deity of Jesus Christ cannot be derived from the Old Testament or understood in the light of it, and only indistinctly can this be said of his pre-existence. It is also very doubtful that the doctrine of the Trinity has any Old Testament roots.

Obbink (*Theologische bezinning op het OT*, p. 19) maintains that there are places in the OT whose messianic character is plain and whose wording and contents almost force us to look to the NT. Unfortunately, he does not mention those passages. On the other hand, he also says that these passages are of little account, and that the OT would still be witness to Christ even if it contained no verses at all referring to Christ's coming in the NT (p. 31). A. R.

Hulst likewise argues that it is the OT as a whole, not each verse in particular, that bears witness to the coming Christ; *Hoe moeten wij het OT uitleggen?*, p. 110.

According to Goppelt, the NT describes the person and work of Jesus Christ with words that refer to God in the OT (Ezek. 34:11ff.; 1:26), but he emphasizes that the deity of Jesus Christ is the antitypical element (the "more than") in the typological relation to OT expectation (*Typos*, pp. 98f., 105, 110-12). Brunner is correct in his thesis that Jesus Christ does not bring God's Word like the prophets, but is the Word himself, so that the divine title "Lord" can be applied to him (*Dogmatik*, I, 22, 26f., 155; Eng. tr., pp. 20, 23f., 148).

Recall that Theodore of Mopsuestia found only less direct prophecies of Christ in the OT; in this connection, note the surprising declaration of the Reformed theologian J. L. Koole that there is little or no express reference to Christ in the OT (*De overname*, p. 4). Nor did Theodore find any intimations in the OT of Christ's divine sonship or of the Trinity; cf. L. Diestel, *Geschichte des AT*, p. 133.

Calvin is very cautious about this. As he put it, the OT saints knew that God had chosen a mediator but not that God's only Son would be this mediator; cf. Schroten, *Christus, der middelaar*, p. 288. Calvin himself found references to Christ's deity only in Zech. 12:10 and Isa. 42:8, and to his two natures in Isa. 7:14; cf. Koopmans, *Het oudkerkelijke dogma in de Reformatie*, pp. 113f. Luther had fewer inhibitions on this score; cf. Bornkamm, *op. cit.*, pp. 87ff.; Eng. tr., pp. 101ff. The Reformers were also very cautious about finding any roots of the doctrine of the Trinity in the OT, Luther less so than Calvin; cf. *ibid.*, pp. 98-103, 165f., 169f.; Eng. tr., pp. 114-20, 195f., 200f.; Koopmans, *op. cit.*, pp. 110-13. What are we to make of Brunner's statement: "It [the Old Testament] does not yet know Him *as* the Trinity, but it does know the Trinity, the true God, who does not unveil the mystery of His threefold being in the Old Testament, but only in the New Testament"; *Offenbarung und Vernunft*, p. 218; Eng. tr., p. 197?

(2) In the New Testament there is a one-sided concentration on guilt and its expiation as effected in Jesus Christ. We have already said that it is indeed possible to see the crucifixion and resurrection in the perspective of the Old Testament. But to reduce the gospel to forgiveness and the Christian life to a life of forgiveness, as Luther does, is hardly in keeping with the Old Testament, though it is possible in the light of the New. Is it really the case that the relation between God and man is

exclusively soteriological? At points the Old Testament perceives dimly that the Servant of God will be a suffering servant who makes atonement by his suffering. But when it thinks of the Servant, and especially when it thinks of the Messiah, it sees primarily the picture of the prophet or even more so the messianic king. Undoubtedly this kingship is to be found in the New Testament as well, but there it is radically grounded in the priestly sacrifice — hence concealed in heaven — and it has a constant bias towards spiritualization. This kingship shakes creation — in marriage, the family, work, culture, and the state (look at passages like Matt. 19:12; Mark 10:21; 10:43; Luke 14:26; I Cor. 7). What does one really do with the world on the basis of the gospel?

One should note the truth of Héring's characterization of the phrase "according to the Scriptures" in I Cor. 15:3f. as "perplexing, for it is not easy to find in the Old Testament precise texts proclaiming the atoning death and the resurrection of a Savior"; *La première épître aux Corinthiens*, p. 134; Eng. tr., p. 158.

Baumgärtel is, I think, correct to say that the OT does not speak christologically even when it speaks of the Messiah, because it understands the Messiah in OT terms (*Verheissung*, p. 69), and also to say that the savior of sinners is nowhere found in the OT (p. 139).

(3) Note how reconciliation takes place according to the New Testament. One might almost say that there is again a tremendous concentration. I have in mind the thought of substitution, which comes out plainly in the New Testament. *One* man is portrayed who takes the place of all men. *One* way of atonement is presented in place of the many forms and ways of atonement known in the Old Testament.[15] The means of salvation becomes the fact of salvation, so that the *eph' hápa* of Golgotha has a factuality and singularity wholly different from that of the Exodus. Above all, it is God himself who makes atonement for man, so that the clear contrast between God and man so characteristic of the Old Testament seems to be done away with in the God-man of the New. From the New Testament standpoint, it is not possible truly to see in the sacrifice at Golgotha an encounter between God and his people.

In this respect the Old Testament is much more human than the New.

The factuality of the act of salvation in the New Testament leads inevitably to dogma. Every confession is a confession of Christ. The heart of Christian doctrine is always the messiahship of Jesus in the historical sense.[16] But how can the Christian understand or even justify its dogma as dogma in terms of the Old Testament?

Goppelt remarks: "How the suffering, death, and resurrection of Jesus accomplished for the many, that is, for all, what the sacrifice of all the martyrs of the old covenant could not accomplish — a new people that is sanctified by God and lives forever — cannot be perceived in terms of the idea of substitution, but only in terms of the unique mystery of the person of Jesus Christ and in faith"; *Typos,* p. 127.
W. J. de Wilde does see an encounter between God and his people in Golgotha: "There is the encounter in the ark, the tabernacle of the body of Christ, the encounter through judgment and death, the encounter to life"; *Het profetische getuigenis,* p. 56.

(4) Consider next the New Testament apostolate. The Old Testament did not envisage the participation of the nations in salvation in this way. For the Old Testament, the salvation in which the nations were to share was accomplished in Israel and in such a way that the nations would come out from themselves, centripetally, to God in Israel. In the New Testament, however, the apostles and with them the church are sent out specially to the nations, from Jerusalem to the ends of the earth. So far as I can see, this is nowhere foreseen in the Old Testament.[17] If one takes seriously the New Testament sayings about the gospel of the kingdom in Galilee, or the sending of Jesus exclusively to the house of Israel, or the setting up of the kingdom "at this time" in Israel (Mark 1:14f.; Matt. 15:24; Acts 1:6), one must even ask whether the centrifugal character of the New Testament apostolate was strictly — or at any rate, originally — willed by God.[18] No matter how much this centrifugal apostolate permeates the whole of the New Testament, it can be regarded as an alien intermezzo, a *mystêrion* that — according to a saying of Paul that reflects its alien

character — was concealed until the present age and is now revealed in factual events (Rom. 16:25f.; Eph. 1:9; 3:1-12; Col. 1:26).

(5) This is linked with the remarkable cutting off of Israel that takes place according to the New Testament, even if only for a specific time. The dominant event of the whole New Testament, the rejection of the Messiah by the chosen people, is not foreseen in the Old Testament. It is this that makes the church the suffering form of the kingdom.[19] Through it the kingship of the Messiah Jesus is, if not spiritualized, at least spiritually concealed. Because of this event the church is alien in the world, only loosely connected with people and state. And because this event of the rejection of the Messiah is suffered to the very utmost, the gospel of Jesus Christ is the gospel of love. In all their depth and horror, man and the world — in the form of the people of Israel that rejects its Messiah — are affirmed in love. It is this affirmation of suffering which even in Isaiah 53 leads to redemption, not (as Buber maintains) repentance, conversion, the power of human freedom.[20] The suffering form of the kingdom of God is accepted. The drama of the world is obviously more dreadful, but the world is also loved much more deeply, than in the Old Testament. One might say that this is the plus element in the gospel as compared with the Torah. But one must also say that this plus has more profound significance. Jesus Christ is not so much the supreme revelation of God — this idea always has an idealistic undertone — as he is the deep point of God's revelation. In him God is more strongly concealed than in Israel and the nations, life and the world. The plus is thus a minus too. The judgment, the great divine vengeance and retribution, the definitive revelation of created reality, and hence the beauty of the world and the full glory of God, are all absent from the gospel of Jesus Christ. Or better, they are so concealed in it that we are taught to sing a note lower — not the high note of divine wrath but the deep note of divine love. Only thus can one assert against Buber and Schoeps that the Redeemer has truly come even though the world is not

yet redeemed. Divine retribution has been visited vicariously on him.[21]

We must remember that the NT itself still belongs to Israel. Jesus is the Messiah and king of Israel. The factuality of the event of salvation is Israelitish and is related to the election of the people of Israel. The cross where Jesus became the Savior of the world is part of the problem of Israel. Guilt and atonement are realities as well as ideas in Israel. The apostles are Israelites. As the twelve they stand for the new Israel, and both geographically and spiritually they go out from Jerusalem to the ends of the earth. In the *ecclesia* the Gentiles are grafted into the stem of Israel. The NT itself is an Israelitish book; this is an important element in its canonicity.

I believe that the NT never says that the people of Israel, even as a biological entity (and how could it have a part in God's dealings without biology?), is definitively rejected. It simply says that the people of Israel is blind and hardened, and indeed with a view to a new development. This development has an eschatological range: it contains the solution to the riddle of the world (Rom. 11:15).

Because the rejection of the Messiah by the chosen people is not foreseen in the OT, it is too simple to state the relation between the OT and the NT as Brunner does (*Offenbarung und Vernunft,* p. 153; Eng. tr., p. 134): "It was only in a people which had thus been prepared that the Christ could be born and understood. The Old Testament revelation is the preparation for the revelation in the New Testament." This is naturally true (the significance of the pedagogical element in God's saving revelation), but the negative side here must be adopted as well as the positive. Baumgärtel goes to the opposite extreme when he says that the people of Israel could not possibly accept Jesus' claim that the basic promise of the OT was fulfilled in him because, taught by prophecy, they linked many earthly historical events that had not taken place with this fulfilment; *Verheissung,* pp. 24f., 27, 57f. In my view this is also too simple an understanding of the relation between the two Testaments.

The idea that the revelation of God in Jesus Christ is higher than that in the OT and the highest in the world (compared with world religions) is current in Christian theology. A. M. Brouwer, for example, writes: "Old and New Testaments constitute one continuous line, but an upward moving line that reaches its peak in Jesus Christ and derives its significance from Him"; *De Bergrede,* p. 263. I should like to dissent from this common Christian view and from the idea that it is axiomatic and self-evident. Granted that there is a history of revelation (for otherwise the NT would be superfluous, and Abraham would know just as much as the modern Christian — as argued by B. J. Oosterhoff, *Het openbaringskarakter van het OT,* pp. 17f.), this history leads to the depths rather than the heights. Israel, Abraham, and the Gentiles do not yet fully know the depths of existence; only Christians learn to know them fully.

Goppelt is right in pointing out that the elements of judgment, divine vengeance, and retribution are "not yet" rather than "no longer" present in the NT situation; *op. cit.*, p. 88. In this respect it must be remembered that retribution is a more radical solution to the problems of existence and the enigma of the world than is love.

We cannot master this fifth incongruity between the Old Testament and the New Testament by resorting to the Lutheran dialectic of the *absconditas veritatis sub contraria specie*. The problem of the relation of the ever new acts of God to his faithfulness and constancy is too great in respect of the relation of the Old Testament and the New to be overcome by even this intrinsically powerful dialectic.

This dialectic is Wolff's way of glossing over the differences between prophetic expectation and evangelical fulfilment; "Der grosse Jesreeltag," p. 103. Bornkamm points out that all Christian tradition has viewed the OT and the NT in terms of pedagogical homogeneity and that Luther was the first to see an element of antithesis in them, just as he understood the word *paidagōgós* in Galatians 3:24f. in terms of a remarkable teacher-pupil relationship characterized by hate. The basic problem here is naturally the interrelation of law and gospel and the question whether the moral law is abrogated or not; *op. cit.*, pp. 214ff.; Eng. tr., pp. 252ff. E. Brunner speaks of a preparatory, provisional, imperfect, nondefinitive revelation that goes before (*Offenbarung und Vernunft*, pp. 100ff., 151ff.; Eng. tr., pp. 81ff., 132ff.), and says: "That which has been fulfilled is the same as that which had been foretold, it is true, because it was the goal of prophecy; but at the same time it is something entirely different, because it is a present reality and no longer merely a vision of the future" (p. 116; Eng. tr., p. 98). This schema is certainly inadequate if we are to do justice to the incongruity indicated.

The only possible way I see of surmounting the difficulty is to declare that we as the Christian church have to accept our position as such in the New Testament, in order that we may then see and acknowledge the Old Testament — which is given to us as the canonical Word of God — not merely as background but rather as horizon.

O. Noordmans argues that "the church does not stand in a regular relation to the OT. The death of Jesus stands between us and this book"; "Het OT en de kerk," p. 100.
Horizon here implies more than background. This will be elucidated and made concrete by the considerations in Chapter Three.

V

The question still remains: how are we, as the Christian church standing in the New Testament in the light of God's act in Jesus Christ, to handle the Old Testament? This leads me to my fifth observation. A renewal of allegorizing may seem to offer a way of assigning an authentic function to the Old Testament in the Christian situation. Can it perhaps be shown with the help of allegorizing that the Old Testament as such already sees Christ?

I believe that we must resist to the last the temptation lurking in this idea. The idea is in fact a temptation, for it seems that allegorizing can solve all the problems of the Christian church in relation to the Old Testament. Bornkamm refers to it as a "very influential late pre-Christian method . . . [that] recommended itself in the first centuries of the church as a contemporary and total solution of the problem."[22] Allegorizing gives the appearance of making it perfectly plain that the Old Testament is wholly and exclusively the book of the Christian church, which can be exploited fully by it alone. With the contemporary ecumenical emphasis in theology, the early church's use of this method adds more attraction to allegorizing.

We must not deviate one hair's breadth at this point. It is bad enough that the allegorical method is really too capricious to warrant even being called a method. In its usual form, it means that at a purely arbitrary point in an Old Testament text or pericope one lights on a word or thought which, by pure association, contains Christ. This word is then taken as the key to the whole text or pericope, which in the light of it seems to be full of Christ. Today, as throughout church history, there are only too many examples of texts of Scripture distorted out of all recognition by this means.[23]

Even worse, allegorizing is not just a method imposed on the Old Testament. It implies further that the Old Testament itself is allegorical by nature — by divine intention of course. He who inspired Scripture inspired it as an allegory. But one cannot speak of God thus. Neither as the God of Israel nor as the Father of Jesus Christ is he known to us as a mysterious conjurer who would amuse himself by conjuring up such an allegory. When God speaks, he normally does so in ordinary, human, earthly terms.

There are also objections relative to God's revelation in Israel. If the Old Testament is an allegory, it follows that God really means something other than what he says. What he says, then, is unimportant. The historical relation of the Old Testament story to this earth is irrelevant. The history of Israel is no longer the true history of God with his people. It is no longer revelation in the full sense of the presence of God. What is particularly seductive is that for allegorizing the terribly difficult problem of the historical reliability of inspired Old Testament Scripture can be solved to everyone's satisfaction. It is more than fatal, however, that the full reality of revelation is dissolved in the process.

The vaporization of the reality of revelation has consequences for the allegorically mediated message of the Old Testament. For this can hardly have a truly historical reality as its content. By way of allegory one cannot find the historical Christ anywhere in the Old Testament. As Sevenster says, allegorizing belongs too much to space and too little to time.[24] It seeks the higher world of eternal truth as expressed in images from the lower world of earthly reality. Allegorically, then, one can find only the eternal Christ in the Old Testament, only the eternal salvation that is imparted to us in some way or other within the Christian church under the ideogram "Christ," even though it be the inner Christ. Allegorizing, then, cannot do justice to its intention of assigning a specific function to the Old Testament in the Christian church, for it inevitably dehistoricizes Christian doctrine and Christian preaching. Hence it is not surprising that the Reformation, with its stress on the historical Christ and the sacrifice at Calvary, banned the allegorical method and concentrated on the literal sense, at most allowing only typology, which it regarded as the *sensus literalis compositus*.

Many in the ecumenical movement impatiently try to attain the consensus in doctrine, liturgy, and order that seems necessary for the desired unity of the church by going back to the undivided church and its traditions and insights. Patristic studies are often pursued as if the fathers were the answer to every contradiction. It is an undoubted fact that the fathers in large measure adopted the allegorical method without hesitation; cf. Goppelt, *Typos*, pp. 6f. But I do not understand how one can argue from this that the Christian church of the twentieth century should meekly use this method. Nevertheless, one finds this idea featured prominently in discussions of and books about ecumenicity. Special note should be taken of the Roman Catholic *nouvelle théologie* in France. The theses of this theology concerning nature and grace and creation and redemption produce a systematic theology that allows for the harmonious integration of the allegorical treatment of the OT. All created reality (and therewith the historical reality of OT history) is understood in the light of the comprehensive order of grace (understood as *elevatio*). In view of this situation in the ecumenical and theological world it is essential that we assemble the most important objections to allegorizing.

In line with the implication that the OT is allegorical by nature, J. L. Koole notes that one of the foundations of the allegorical method in the early church was the principle of the obscurity of scripture, specifically of Holy Scripture; *De overname van het OT*, pp. 163ff.

Bornkamm says that "to Luther God showed himself in the Old Testament through an event, not through figurative hints"; *op. cit.*, p. 158; Eng. tr., p. 187. This was connected for Luther with his sacramental teaching. He understood the sacraments not cultically but as signs annexed by God to the Word of promise in historical reality (cf. p. 172; Eng. tr., pp. 202f.). *Ex historia aedificanda est fides* — "faith rests upon history" (p. 77; Eng. tr., p. 91) — in the sense that the history of Israel, taken literally, offers examples by which we may find comfort and strength in our own inner history.

Luther's objections to allegorizing were (1) that it destroys the true history (the history of Israel as the history of Christ and faith) (Bornkamm, *op. cit.*, p. 211; Eng. tr., p. 249); (2) that it misses the sense of Christ in Scripture (p. 76; Eng. tr., p. 89); and (3) that it robs faith of its certainty, since allegorizing is made up of purely human conjectures (pp. 77f.; Eng. tr., pp. 90f.). It is true that, in particular before 1525, Luther himself allegorized, because Scripture itself does. But this was only as a game that gives color to preaching, never as true exegesis, except when the text yields no usable sense (pp. 79ff.; Eng. tr., pp. 92ff.). Always it must be "directed to a goal which was clearly and unequivocally determined by the literal sense of other Scripture passages" (p. 79; Eng. tr., p. 92). Luther rejected allegorical exegesis only in order to be able to expound the OT christocentrically or even christologically (*sensus literalis propheticus*). In so doing he did more violence to the historical and factual content of the OT than had ever been done by the fourfold scheme, which in the first instance honored the pure literal sense.

Brunner points out that the allegorical method softens and indeed invalidates the literalistic theory of authority that is strictly implied by the idea of verbal inspiration (which the church took over from Judaism); *Dogmatik*, I, 113f.; Eng. tr., 107f. Behind this problem of historical reliability is concealed an even more serious problem, namely, that of the purpose of concretely historical and earthly facts as elements in revelation. From Origen to Erasmus the OT had to be taken allegorically because the literal meaning seemed to be "quite senseless, indeed, often enough, repulsive and ridiculous"; Bornkamm, *op. cit.*, p. 214; Eng. tr., p. 252.

According to Cullmann, "the unexpressed presupposition of all purely allegorical explanation is that in the books to be interpreted the line of development in time has no importance, but that on the contrary these books contain hidden, *timeless* truths, and that accordingly, in our case, everything that the gospels report is without exception to be found also in the Old Testament, if only one knows how to use rightly the allegorical method. Thus, fundamentally, the New Testament writings are made disposable in advance. The Old Testament already contains the 'life of Jesus.' By this means not only is the redemptive history that the Old Testament contains dissolved as such, but even the unique incarnation of Jesus Christ and the unique apostolic preaching of this incarnation are no longer taken seriously"; *op. cit.*, p. 117; Eng. tr., p. 133.

Nevertheless, if we are not careful, another problem arises here that can become a good plea in vindication of allegorizing. At issue is one of the basic questions of theological and religious knowledge in general. The question is sometimes asked in modern theology whether allegorizing should not be recognized as a legitimate interpretation of the Bible, at least in the Christian church.[25] This basic question has to do with the problem of the relation between the outer intellectual knowledge and the inner spiritual knowledge of the words and acts of God. There is a great deal of difference between hearing only the outer side of the words and pictures and being aware as well of what is really being said and done by God in these words and pictures, that is, of what he is truly seeking to express in them.

This problem can be called the problem of the inner Word, though not in the sense in which that expression is ordinarily used. We are not concerned merely with the question of how the Word that comes from the outer world (of history and society) penetrates into man, finds an echo there, takes shape, and becomes truth within. The problem must also be seen from the opposite side, where it seems to be a much bigger problem, as was discovered by Jodocus van Lodensteyn, one of the leaders of Reformed pietism in the Netherlands. He pointed out that what is at issue is the Word that is inward in God, the purpose, meaning, and intention that are in the heart of God, which he seeks to express towards the children of men when he addresses them and deals with them in all historical reality.[26] We have encountered this problem several times already. In connection with the doctrine of Scripture it is to this effect: Should we or should we not exegete the Scriptures with a view to, or in the light of, their primary author? Once it is perceived that the task of theological scholarship is to take seriously God's revelation in the world, one simply cannot ignore this problem.

It may be pointed out in this connection that modern hermeneutical discussion puts too strongly the question of God's Word in man, with an existential reference, and pays too little attention to the fact that the Word is also the Word in God. The reason is perhaps to be sought in a doctrine of the trinity that has been christologically constricted.

This central problem of the inner Word (in the full theological sense, and not just the anthropological) applies not only to the Old Testament but equally to the New. Here too the question of what is truly present in God's heart and what he is seeking to express in revelation arises. This is not perceived merely by repeating and retelling the words and facts of the New Testament.

But how can one attain to and comprehend the purpose of God? Is there any possibility of a mysterious, supernatural way? Or must one say that the scholarly, historico-critical and philological work of exegesis should have this as its goal? At any rate, one cannot move on here from a literal to an allegorical sense of the words. God has expressed the inner Word in outer words. So it is there that we must find the heart of the matter.

Perhaps we are forced to say that scholarship alone is not enough at this point. Regeneration is quite indispensable if we are to know God and to understand him in his words and acts. True exegesis is thus possible only in and by the Holy Spirit. This, then, is *the* true exegesis. But if so, we have here the fundamental problem of all exegesis. Exegesis as a discipline of theological scholarship is possible only in the sphere of a Christianized culture. (This does not mean that it has to be ecclesiastical scholarship, for faith and reason can enter into marriage.)

On the other side, however, we should not lose sight of the fact that history and letter, *pragma* and *gramma,* play a role in the *pneuma*. Exegesis, if it takes place by and in the Holy Spirit, will make radical reference to the letter and the literal sense. In relation to this very problem allegorizing shoots far beyond the mark. Even at best it winds up with an exclusively immanent Trinitarian Spirit who has not entered into *pragma* and *gramma*. In fact, it may very well wind up merely with the inwardness of man.

VI

Much more decisive (this leads me to my sixth observation) is the new attempt being made today to use the typological method.

Unless I am deceived, the *Biblischer Kommentar* on which a team is now seriously at work will take this path in an effort to

make the OT again fruitful for the preaching of Christ in the modern
world, on the basis of the historico-critical method and within that
framework.

G. von Rad writes, in his essay "Typologische Auslegung des AT":
"Whether the term 'typology' should be retained for what is outlined
in this essay, whether it is perhaps too heavily freighted, whether it
is here stretched by us much beyond its older sense, so that it will
make discussion harder rather than easier, may well be asked. The
word has, in fact, been used because it seemed honest to begin by
making fresh contact with the ancient hermeneutical tradition, which
in relation to the witness of the Old Testament always seems to be
more relevant than our theological spiritualizing. If the concept
should prove untenable, it would be helpful if friends and foes alike
could show precisely why" (p. 33).

A careful analysis of the meaning of the concept "typology"
as used today yields the following results:

(1) Typology sets in relation the historical facts of the past
on the one hand and later historical facts on the other.[27]

Goppelt regards this as very important: "The basic difference
between allegory and typology is well expressed in J. Gerhard's
definition: *'Typus consistit in factorum collatione. Allegoria occu-
patur non tam in factis, quam in ipsis concionibus, e quibus doc-
trinam utilem et reconditam depromit'* " (*Typos*, p. 18). "The object
of typological interpretation can only be historical facts, that is,
persons, actions, events and institutions, and words and descriptions
only to the extent that they deal with the above" (p. 20).

(2) The two kinds of facts between which a typological
relation exists are both God's contingent self-presentation.[28]
Consequently the historical facts of the past are wholly real
and wholly God's work,[29] and as such they are important for
revelation. In other words, the incarnation is not the only
revelation.[30]

(3) There is a remarkable connection between what precedes
and what comes later. This is to be seen especially in eschatological contexts, where some of the features of the first time
recur in the last time, though with only a slight suggestion of
a cyclical sense.[31] What holds good eschatologically also holds
good historically, in the whole history of Israel and conse-

quently in the relation between the history of Jesus Christ[32] (and not only of Jesus Christ but also of the church as his body) and the Old Testament. One constantly finds parallels, evident analogies, outlines of Christ, prefigurings. This is not a case of mere recurrence. For, on the one hand, there is an element of continuation and completion — the continuation and completion of God's dealings — so that this element is not just pragmatic, human, and historical; on the other hand there are also elements of development — inasmuch as the words and acts of God are always greater and more complete — and even of antithesis, in which the antitype is given a place along with the type.[33] This thought perhaps embraces the incongruity between the Old and New Testaments that we discussed above.

Goppelt has found that in Palestinian Judaism at the time of the Tannaites the typological mode of thought and typological interpretation of the OT occurred only in eschatological contexts; *Typos*, p. 34.

The relevance of the OT to the church *as Christ's body* is not much considered today. E. Stauffer shows some interest in this problem; cf. *Die Theologie des NT*, secs. 21, 37, 46. G. von Rad mentions it briefly: "The reference of Old Testament statements to the New Testament is not limited, however, to the person and life of Christ, but extends to the total Christ-event attested in the New Testament, including the ecclesiological aspect"; "Typologische Auslegung," p. 32.

In my view the problem that arises here cannot be passed over. The church as Christ's body is just as important as Christ himself. If one pursues and takes seriously the typological method, sooner or later he has to find a typological place for church history in Holy Scripture, which involves an enormous extension of typology. Cocceius took this way; cf. Schrenk, *Gottesreich und Bund*, pp. 209ff., 219ff. F. A. Lampe finally discovered all church history in the Bible; cf. Snijders, *Friedrich Adolph Lampe*, pp. 24, 74, 99, 104. This use of Holy Scripture is better called typological than allegorical. H. Witsius seeks the *spiritual* bearing of biblical sayings rather than the *historical*, whether general or ecclesiastical; cf. J. van Genderen, *Herman Witsius*, p. 123. The course of the individual soul is thus described in the Bible. This psychological use of the Bible is, in principle, not very different from the application of it to church history. Once one seeks something more than the local and temporal meaning of the content of the Bible, all these possibilities open up; and they all present equal difficulties. Otherwise, one has to turn to the allegorical method, which seeks an eternal *reality* in the Bible, or the rational method, which seeks an eternal *truth;* and this comes to the same thing in principle.

G. von Rad says, "New in the New Testament is the application of these theological thought-forms to a book, to the canon of the Old Testament, while this theological and eschatological thinking in terms of analogies was, as we have seen, very largely prepared by the Old Testament's understanding of itself"; "Typologische Auslegung," p. 19. "We see rather in the history effected by God's Word — both in judgments and acts of salvation — the Christ-event of the New Testament already prefigured" (pp. 19f., 31). This recognition of types in the OT is based on the belief that it is the same God who has left his marks there. Cf. H. W. Wolff, "Der grosse Jesreeltag," p. 102, for evident analogies, parallels, outlines of the Christ-event.

(4) This typological connection is with the Old Testament as a whole, not just with the messianic prophecies, for example, but with everything in which God's action is attested.[34] On the question whether a typological relation is to be seen in historical and archaeological details as well, different views have been expressed. Certainly there is a readiness to go far beyond the old Reformed rule that we are to treat as types only those things that God himself has shown to be such.[35]

"Typological interpretation," according to Von Rad, "is concerned only with the witness to the divine dealings, not with the correspondence of historical, cultural, or archaeological details common to the Old and New Testaments. It has to keep to the kerygma in view, not to details in the narrative with whose help alone the kerygma is established"; "Typologische Auslegung," pp. 31f. Furthermore, he concludes that there are a number of texts that record history alone without commentary; one should not try to find a meaning in everything (pp. 32f.). On the other hand, H. W. Wolff argues that "it cannot be ruled out that types of the day of Christ may be seen even in details of the Day of Jezreel"; "Der grosse Jesreeltag," p. 103.

(5) The question is raised whether this typological connection is a later one, or whether we have to allow for the fact that God established it from the very outset, so that the Old Testament may be treated as an "intimation," a "prior, pre-

figurative depiction," all oriented to the coming of Jesus Christ.[36] The latter possibility introduces the exegetical problem of the primary author and whether exegesis should be in the light of his intention. But it also raises again the fatal possibility, already mentioned and criticized in relation to allegorizing, that we have to regard God as a conjurer.

Luther tried to avoid these Antiochene notions of a prefigurative anticipation of the Christ-event and of figurative intimations on the grounds that (1) the words of the OT would then assume a double sense; and (2) he wanted to have Christ's presence in the OT understood in terms of historical actuality; Bornkamm, *op. cit.*, pp. 212-19; Eng. tr., pp. 249-58.

Baumgärtel rightly points out that the typological method leads back to the doctrine of inspiration; "Der Dissensus," p. 305. H. W. Wolff writes: "Since he [Christ] is the final word of God, the Old Testament Word is to be interpreted in terms of the New Testament analogy"; "Der grosse Jesreeltag," p. 102. According to Cullmann, finding the OT witness to Christ means "to learn, upon the basis of our knowledge concerning the incarnate and crucified Christ, how to understand the past events of redemptive history as preparation for the incarnation and the cross"; *op. cit.*, p. 119; Eng. tr., p. 135.

(6) The possibility must be conceded that the authors and readers of the Old Testament text did not understand what that text actually meant, but this thought is parried at once by the question whether they really understood what God was directly saying to them and doing among them.[37]

W. H. Gispen emphasizes that he was really present in these and appeals for support to the unity of the Testaments and of revelation; *De Christus in het OT*, pp. 36f. Baumgärtel stresses the importance of this problem: the OT does not regard itself as a collection of types; Israel under the old covenant knew nothing of types; if, consequently, there are typological features in OT history they did not help believers in Israel; thus the types were given only for Christians; so it is difficult to see why they were necessary; cf. *Verheissung*, pp. 78f., 139f.; "Der Dissensus," p. 304.

(7) We must consider whether we as Christian theologians have to understand the earlier in terms of the later, the Old

Testament in terms of the New. The argument is that no real sense could be made of a text until the typological key was found in a larger context.[38] It is believed, however, that typology cannot be made a method in the strict sense. And indeed, where does it lead except to a homiletical use and hortatory application?[39]   Is typology really an aid to genuine exegesis? Does the Old Testament really tell us in this way anything about Christ that we do not already know from the New Testament?

G. von Rad underlines the inability of typology to shed light on detailed philological and historical problems. Yet, he argues, typology must not be dropped from historico-critical work, since even historically "better exegesis will often result on the basis of theology, and this ultimately means on the basis of faith in Christ"; "Typologische Auslegung," p. 32. As far as the question of method is concerned, Von Rad writes that "for the application of typological interpretation to individual texts, no academic norm can be given; it cannot be regulated hermeneutically, but takes place in the freedom of the Holy Spirit" (p. 33). In my view this is basically wrong. Dogmatically it rests on an incorrect doctrine of the Spirit. H. W. Wolff adds: "This kind of typological exposition in terms of salvation history cannot be made into a true method"; "Der grosse Jesreeltag," pp. 97, 104. Baumgärtel is horrified and angered by such statements; "Ohne Schlüssel?", pp. 413-21.

(8) Reference is made, of course, to Jesus Christ as "the final end of the ways of God" with his people Israel, and consequently to Christ's "secret presence" in the Old Testament.[40]
  At this point some critical observations may be made.
  First of all, it seems to me that on a typological view one is uncritically guided by the implicit belief of Christian tradition and the explicit principle of Barth's *Dogmatics* that Jesus Christ is the final end of the ways of God with his people Israel. But is God really concerned about Jesus Christ in Israel? Or is he concerned about Israel in Jesus Christ? Or, one might equally well ask, is God really concerned about the people of Israel in the nations of the earth or is he concerned about the nations of the earth in Israel? Indeed, we must press the question to the bitter end: in creation is God really concerned about

grace, the covenant, salvation, or is he rather in salvation concerned about created reality, that it may stand before his
presence?

It is important to see that Baumgärtel takes the side of his oppo-
nents at this decisive point: "In the Old Covenant God has us in
view, since under the promise in Christ we experience and know
that in his basic promise God had in view its fulfilment in Jesus
Christ"; *Verheissung,* p. 48. "But the Old Testament is certainly
oriented to Jesus Christ with its 'I am the Lord thy God.' This
basic promise is the promise of God, that is, it is given in order
that it might be fulfilled in Jesus Christ" (p. 67).

Our concern here is with the basic structure of systematic
theology. If everything is oriented to Christ, the Old Testament is necessarily full of Christ and must have a place in the
Christian church. This must have been the intention of the
primary author, and one is justified in speaking of preliminary
intimations. What fills the heart is expressed by the lips. If
God's heart is really so full of Jesus Christ, then in the inspiration of the Old Testament he lets slip — if one might put it
thus — a permanent typological reference to Jesus Christ.

In passing I should like to note that there is no exclusive connection between the doctrine of inspiration and typological exegesis; cf.
Baumgärtel, *Verheissung,* p. 304. The question whether God speaks
in the OT (cf. Chapter One) is not the same question as whether his
concern is with Jesus Christ.

I should like, however, to call into question the correctness
of this entire point of view. The incarnation is exclusively
motivated by sin,[41] and the crucifixion took place because
Israel rejected its Messiah. In no sense is super-nature added
to nature in Jesus Christ. What takes place in him is "simply"
that guilt is expiated and all being is saved before God's
presence. God's concern is for us who are saved by him, not
for the one who saves us. We are not men in order that we
might be Christians; we are Christians in order that we might
be men. Undoubtedly everything revolves around Jesus Christ,
since the enigma of guilt is solved in his sacrifice. But this

should not lead us to the false deduction that the whole concern is with Jesus Christ. The Spirit embraces more than the Messiah does.[42] Sanctification is greater than reconciliation. The Son will one day hand back the kingdom of God to his Father. From the very first everything is oriented to this. There is concentration — from the nations to the nation, from the nation to the remnant, from the remnant to the individual. But this concentration becomes expansion — from the Messiah to the Spirit, from the Spirit to the conscience, from the conscience to the state, from the state to the cosmos.[43] If I may put it briefly and sharply, Jesus Christ is an emergency measure that God postponed as long as possible (cf. Matt. 21:33-46). Hence we must not try to find him fully in the Old Testament, even though as Christian theologians we investigate the Old Testament in orientation to God.

A basic thesis of the Reformation in opposition to Rome was that original righteousness was natural rather than supernatural. From a biblical standpoint this was an enormous step forward. The thesis is also of incalculable importance for a proper attitude to life and affirmation of the world. But it means that one can no longer see in Christ's work the addition of a higher life to created life. And this has important implications for the relation of Christ to the OT.

It seems to me to be vitally important for present-day theology to avoid Docetism in its pneumatology. The sequence, Spirit — conscience — state — cosmos, is to be understood in the light of this concern.

The thesis that Jesus Christ was an emergency measure relates to the incarnate Son rather than the eternal Son. Thus the doctrine of the Trinity is not affected by it, and it has nothing whatever to do with Subordinationism. Quite the contrary — for only thus can one achieve a sober view of the Trinity. Theopaschitism, which is so strongly present in modern theology, violates the mystery of the Trinity; G. C. Berkouwer finds this theopaschitism in Barth; cf. *De triomf der genade,* pp. 294-324; Eng. tr., 297-327. One must see Christ as mediator to be able to think of God as Trinity. It is naturally impossible to pursue here this question, which belongs essentially to systematic theology. But it is most important to see that this is all at issue when we deal with the problem of the OT in the Christian church.

Bornkamm makes it quite clear that Luther's view that Christ himself was historically present in the OT is rooted directly in his

Christology; cf. Bornkamm, *op. cit.*, pp. 173-76, 220, 226; Eng. tr., pp. 204-07, 259, 265f.

In the second place, I believe that one should use the principle of typology much more cautiously. In particular, the *a posteriori* character of typological connections should be much more strongly recognized. We agree that God's plan and purpose were there before the foundation of the world; but, enclosed in the heart of God, they were a mystery concealed until the days of the apostles. Only now are they disclosed in all their factuality, to our astonishment. That Gentiles as well as Jews have access to the kingdom of God as the kingdom of Christ surprises the men of the New Testament. They find this hard to accept.

Not until later could one say that it was all there in the Old Testament. The disciples saw it only in and after the resurrection, according to John's Gospel (2:22; 20:9). Reformed dogmatics argues that we may not see all of God's hand during the game, only those cards he himself discloses. Only that is a type which is specifically declared to be such by God himself.

It is true that even according to the New Testament the Old Testament speaks a great deal about Jesus Christ and the salvation manifested in him. Gispen argues on this basis that to seek Christ in the Old Testament is to do what Jesus himself did, what the apostles did in their preaching, and what the authors of the New Testament did in their writing. It is of decisive importance, he argues, that Jesus himself saw in Isaiah 53 the statement of a divine imperative.[44] Nevertheless, the decisive question is what the New Testament means by this. Do we not have to take it spiritually? And in this context does not "taking it spiritually" mean that what the Old Testament says about Jesus Christ again takes place in concrete reality: he is born of a woman, born under the law (Gal. 4:4); he took his place under the total structure of God's dealings with his people Israel as this structure is described in the law and the prophets; and it was all fulfilled in him paradigmatically because he was the incarnate Son of God?

An illuminating example is Matt. 2:15, which finds in Jesus a fulfilment of the prophetic saying of Hos. 11:1, which is clearly referring to the Exodus. The text is not speaking of the Messiah Jesus; it is speaking of Israel. It is speaking of Israel as it finds (found) itself in the hands of God. But the Messiah King, Jesus, places himself under all the words of God, and they are also fulfilled in him. This takes place in the actuality of occurrence. In this sense these words refer to him also.

To say that this fulfilment in Christ is "paradigmatic" means, among other things, that it was once for all. Thus, it has decisive content; it took place with saving power. It is thus paradigmatic in the sense that, in him, it is fulfilled in his body and in the nations of the earth.

This is how I would understand the idea that the Old Testament is fulfilled in Jesus Christ. What is meant is on the one hand that the Old Testament is put into effect in him and on the other that it speaks about him because it is fulfilled in him, and not *vice versa*. Hence we no longer look for intimations of Jesus Christ and his work in the Old Testament. Both exegetically and homiletically we can approach the Old Testament as the witness to revelation by and in God's history with Israel.

Standing in the Christian church, which is given its position in the New Testament, we know at least that everything in the Old Testament is true because it is also — "also" in an incomparable way — fulfilled in Jesus Christ. In him it has all been put into effect and is Yea and Amen.

Third, it must be considered that the Old Testament is fulfilled in Jesus Christ especially in its central question, namely, that of guilt and expiation, of slaying and making alive, of love as the untroubled relation between the two — God and man. Only in the light of fulfilment here is it also fulfilled in respect of other questions.

The monarchy is not reestablished for Israel in and by Jesus Christ (Acts 1:6). It is set up for Israel only in its core, the offering of reconciliation. In this light it is readily seen why Luther found many things even in the canonical Scriptures that bore no relation to the core of the Bible, the command and the promise; cf. Bornkamm, *op. cit.*, p. 160; Eng. tr., p. 190. If one approaches the OT from the NT with the schema of law and gospel and the belief that the truth of forgiveness is the main concern, this will mean an impossible restriction in the field of vision, as J. Hempel points out (quoted in J. Klevinghaus, *Die theologische Stellung der apostolischen Väter,* pp. 149f.). The Reformation led us astray in this respect. Cf. also G. von Rad, "Verheissung," pp. 409f. H. Bornkamm clings yet to the Reformation view; *op. cit.,* pp. 223f.; Eng. tr., pp. 262f.

This means that in the Old Testament what is to be typologically related to Jesus Christ is not the only or even the most important concern. Hence one cannot exclusively seek Christ and the *sóma Christoú* in the Old Testament. One must rather seek typological light for the *eschaton,* for Israel, the world, and God himself. The Old Testament is and remains the true Bible.[45] In it God has made known himself and the secret that he has with the world. All goodness and also all truth and beauty — the fully redemptive knowledge of being — shines out before us in this book. It is the book of humanity. This perspective is of immense significance for the exegesis that takes place under the sign of typology. It means that both exegetically and homiletically one must continually begin afresh and remain occupied with the text of the Old Testament itself. One should not seek only that which sets forth Christ; one should not regard the gospel of Jesus Christ as the only standard of evaluation nor as the only hermeneutical key in interpretation of the Old Testament.[46] Heart and life, state and history, as they are fashioned in the apostolic process of Christianizing, are also standards and keys. In all this, the Old Testament itself remains the canonical Word of God, and it constantly confronts us with its own authority.

In none of its forms does paganism achieve pure humanity, for it forces man into a divine context of being (reason, state, cosmos); the New Testament violently restricts humanity with its concepts of incarnation and substitution.

Bornkamm points out that a great deal of mischief has been wrought by Luther's idea of seeking only that which sets forth Christ in the OT. It is illegitimate to deduce from it that certain Christian thoughts or even certain lines that lead to Jesus Christ can or should be found in the OT. In Luther's view the expression means that Christ himself may be found truly and historically in the OT. Cf. Bornkamm, *op. cit.*, pp. 82f., 103f., 128f., 169ff., 216; Eng. tr., pp. 96f., 120f., 150ff., 200ff., 255f. As I see it, historico-critical work has now made this a complete impossibility.

Footnotes to Chapter Two

[1]Cullmann, *Christus und die Zeit*, p. 116; Eng. tr., p. 132, states that "the question that has recently been raised by Wilhelm Vischer's book on the witness of the Old Testament to Christ [*Das Christuszeugnis*] is actually a primitive Christian problem."

[2]Zimmerli, "Verheissung und Erfüllung," p. 43. This is a central point in the discussion with Buber on the interpretation of the OT. Cf. Kraus, "Gespräch mit M. Buber," pp. 72-74.

[3]Goppelt, *Typos*, p. 43; Von Rad, "Typologische Auslegung," pp. 23f.

[4]Zimmerli, *op. cit.*, p. 53.

[5]Cf. Hellbardt, "Christus, das Telos des Gesetzes."

[6]Zimmerli, *op. cit.*, pp. 53ff.

[7]Cf. Cullmann, *Christus und die Zeit.*

[8]Zimmerli, *op. cit.*, p. 53.

[9]Schoeps, *Theologische Literaturzeitung*, February 1954, p. 74.

[10]Von Rad, in *TWNT*, I, 566f.; *TDNT*, I, 568f.

[11]Zimmerli, *op. cit.*, pp. 44, 46.

[12]Miskotte points out that the modern Jewish philosophy of religion understands or interprets Israel and its faith as well as the OT in terms of this idea of correlation; *Het wezen der joodsche religie*, pp. 448ff.

[13]Zimmerli, *op. cit.*, p. 46.

[14]A striking example of this is to be found in Psalm 95; cf. De Groot, *De Psalmen*, pp. 202ff.

[15]Vriezen, *Hoofdlijnen der theologie van het OT*, pp. 213-44.

[16]Barth, *Das Bekenntnis*, p. 9.

[17]Cf. Blauw, *Goden en Menschen.*

[18]Hoedemaker speaks of the "destruction of the kingdom in Galilee"; *Handboek voor het NT*, pp. 261ff.

[19]Hoedemaker, *op. cit.*; *Handboek voor het onderwijs in het OT*, p. 55. Cf. Scheers, *Philippus Jacobus Hoedemaker*, p. 228; Haitjema, *De richtingen in de Nederlandse Hervormde Kerk*, p. 164. One has to consider this mode of suffering and the cross if one says with Baumgärtel that the NT Christian has fellowship with God, and if one is to see here a characteristic of the NT in contrast to the OT; *Verheissung*, pp. 51f.

[20]Cf. the discussion between Kraus and Buber, *loc. cit.*, pp. 76f. This is the core of the gospel of Jesus Christ. Luther brought this to light again with his concepts of *agnitio peccati* and *iustificatio Dei passiva.*

[21]Cf. Kraus, *ibid.*, p. 77.

[22]Bornkamm, *Luther und das AT*, pp. 210f.; Eng. tr., p. 249.

[23]For a full collection of the crassest examples from the early church cf. Koole, *De overname, passim.*

[24]Sevenster, *De Christologie van het NT*, pp. 250ff.

[25]For example, Van Niftrik, building on the presuppositions of Barth's theology, makes a plea for the indispensability of allegorizing; "De verborgen zin der Schrift," pp. 41-59.

[26]Van Lodensteyn, *Beschouwinge van Zion*, pp. 23-25, 239, 249; cf. on this my essay "De bevinding in de prediking."

[27]Von Rad, "Typologische Auslegung," pp. 21ff. (cf. his correction in "Verheissung," p. 411: Hegel with his philosophy of history had more influence than the Enlightenment in shifting interest away from the concrete facts to generally valid truths).

[28]Goppelt, *Typos*, p. 70.

[29]*Ibid.*, p. 18.

[30]Oosterhoff, *Het openbaringskarakter van het OT*, p. 18.

[31]Von Rad, "Typologische Auslegung," pp. 18f.; cf. Goppelt, *op. cit.*, p. 43.

[32]*Ibid.*, pp. 71ff.

[33]Von Rad, "Typologische Auslegung," p. 20 (development from type to antitype); Goppelt, *op. cit.*, pp. 18f. (prefigurations, i.e., types of coming and greater and more complete facts), p. 71 (continuation and completion), p. 88 (not just development, but the contrast between stages in salvation history).

[34]Von Rad, "Typologische Auslegung," p. 31.

[35]Heppe, *Die Dogmatik der evangelisch-reformierten Kirche*, p. 275; Eng. tr., p. 403; Van Genderen, *Herman Witsius*, p. 120.

[36]Goppelt, *op. cit.*, p. 18 (divinely given prefigurations); Zimmerli, "Verheissung und Erfüllung," p. 58 (that faith in Christ later finds in the OT a book full of genuine references to Christ); Wolff, "Der grosse Jesreeltag," p. 102 (prophetic depiction); Cullmann, *Christus und die Zeit*, p. 119; Eng. tr., p. 135 (the view that the whole of the OT salvation history is oriented to the incarnation).

[37]Von Rad, "Typologische Auslegung," pp. 26f., 31.

[38]Wolff, "Der grosse Jesreeltag," p. 104.

[39]There is a striking example of this in Gispen, *De Christus in het OT*.

[40]Kraus, "Gespräch mit M. Buber," p. 77.

[41]Berkouwer, *Het werk van Christus*, chapter II, pp. 17-33; Eng. tr., pp. 19-34. If I am right this thesis is no longer affirmed by Karl Barth in his *Kirchliche Dogmatik*, IV/1.

[42]For explicit development of this thesis, cf. my *De vervulling van de wet*.

[43]Stauffer, *Theologie des NT, passim:* universal history.

[44]Gispen, *op. cit.*, pp. 6, 32.

[45]I have defended the thesis that the OT is the true Bible and the NT its explanatory glossary in *Religie en politiek*, pp. 123-49.

[46]Vriezen, *Hoofdlijnen der theologie van het OT*, p. 76: "Christ is for theology generally as also for the assessment of the Old Testament, the norm of truth."

CHAPTER THREE

THE NECESSITY OF THE OLD TESTAMENT FOR THE CHRISTIAN CHURCH

In conclusion, we shall consider why and in what sense the Christian church cannot do without the Old Testament but must regard it as a canonical Word that is at least given to it too, and how it must use it as such. In doing this, we shall assemble the results of our previous deliberations and arrange them from this new standpoint. We shall try to embrace the whole material with the help of six concepts, and we shall end by discussing two problems. The six concepts are *legitimation, foundation, interpretation, illustration, historicization,* and *eschatologization;* the two problems are the Old Testament as a special canon in the Christian church and the Old Testament as the book of the people of Israel.

I

According to the insight of the Christian community, which we also accept, the Old Testament is necessary for the Christian church first of all as a *legitimation* of Jesus as the Christ. By showing that what Jesus does and what takes place in him are in harmony with the structure of God's relation to his people and his dealings with them, the Old Testament also shows that he is sent by God. In particular, when he makes the offering of atonement, Jesus is in agreement with that upon which the Old Testament progressively focuses things.

In this sense the law and the prophets bear witness to the gospel of Jesus Christ (Rom. 3:21).[1] This means not so much that they see and describe Jesus Christ in advance, but rather that in the suit between Jesus Christ and the apostles on the one side and the people of Israel on the other, they throw their weight in the scales to show that Jesus Christ was in fact sent by God.

As witness to Christ in this sense, the Old Testament indeed has permanent significance in the Christian situation. From the Christian standpoint everything depends on the messiahship of Jesus, and a decision can be reached on this messiahship only when the question is raised and answered whether Jesus really does the works of God. What these works are, however, can be ascertained only with the help of the Old Testament. This is why Jesus refers to the Old Testament as the witness in which the Father bears witness to him (John 5:32ff.).[2] This is also why John the Baptist is referred to these works, though Jesus adds, "Blessed is he, whosoever shall not be offended in me" (Matt. 11:2ff.).

Lk. 7:23

The importance of this idea — that the OT functions in the Christian church as legitimation — may be seen in a broad and fundamental context when one considers that God has chosen Israel to be the agent of his revelation in the world. He wished also to be present in word and act among the Gentiles. "Naturally the call had to come from where God had given his word, from a prophet of Israel"; Bornkamm, *Luther und das AT*, p. 226; Eng. tr., p. 265. The salvation of the world is of the Jews (John 4:22) even when it comes in the form of the person and work of Jesus Christ. At issue here is the continuity in God's saving action, the identity, indeed, of the God of the OT and the God of the NT.

Vriezen's statement is most inadequate: "Nevertheless the Old Testament can rightly be called witness to Christ inasmuch as it confirms the truth of the saving figure of Christ. . . . He was unmistakably the only true Son of Israel who took the message of the prophets with full seriousness"; *Hoofdlijnen der theologie van het OT*, pp. 71f.

Baumgärtel (*Verheissung,* pp. 72ff., 78, 83, 97, 150) argues that the legitimation of Jesus as the Christ was necessary only in the NT and for the Jews, but that it does not have the slightest significance for Christians. One can, it seems to me, sustain this thesis only if one recognizes in the process of salvation no more than the dimension of the personal decision of faith and the actuality of the church. If it is once seen that the Christian faith is oriented to an historical fact, and is thus essentially enmeshed in the historical process, the legitimation of Jesus as the Christ remains an important matter. This aspect is reflected in the discussion between church and synagogue. In particular, the problem of legitimation looms large where there is a proper appreciation of the role of the people of Israel in God's plan for the world in past, present, and future.

The Old Testament, then, is witness, but it is no more. It is not judge. For there is a plus in the New Testament as compared with the Old. At the center this is the deity of Jesus. The Old Testament also has its own plus as compared with the New. At the center this is the kingdom of God. Thus there is certainly no full congruity between the Old Testament and the New. They differ at essential points. But the deity of Jesus and the kingdom of God combine — in one way or another — in the messiahship of Jesus. And here the Old Testament comes forward with its legitimation.

The Messiah had to suffer all these things and enter into his glory (Luke 24:26). This divine constraint may be seen in the Old Testament. But it has as such a deeper root in the counsel of God. The counsel of God and the Word of God must not be confused. The Torah does not stand above God. It simply bears witness — from the sidelines as it were — to God's action in his history with the people of Israel and to his new action in Jesus Christ. Only thus can one satisfactorily explain the remarkable fact that on the one hand the New Testament does not advocate a book religion but is wholly oriented to the Messiah and the Spirit as (new) figures in history, and yet on the other hand it so diligently seeks the light that the Old Testament sheds on this new event.

In this modest but vital role, however, the Old Testament has and maintains decisive significance. For it has something decisive to say on the historical question whether Jesus was (and is) the Messiah.

H. F. Kohlbrügge emphasizes especially this first point; cf. *Wozu das AT?, passim.* For the Jews — and also for the early Christians — deviation from Moses and the prophets was blasphemy (p. 21). For them the supreme authority was not Jesus and what took place with him, but Scripture (p. 86). In the NT it is constantly shown from the OT that Jesus is the Christ (e.g., John 1:46; 5:45; Acts 2; 17:11; 28:23).

II

To sharpen our focus on the problem, let us now consider the opposite side of the matter. The Old Testament is also indispensable to the Christian church because it has received in Jesus Christ the *foundation* of all that is at issue in it.

In Jesus Christ all the promises of God are Yea and Amen (II Cor. 1:20; cf. Rev. 3:14). He is the true object of all signs,[3] the body of all shadows, the true image of things (Col. 2:17; Heb. 10:1). In him everything between God and his people — and consequently everything between God and man and God and the world — has been validated (Rom. 15:8; II Cor. 1:21; Heb. 2:2f.). Finally, in him and his sacrifice the kingdom of God has acquired a firm place on earth.

This could not happen without extreme emergency measures, without a certain compulsion from God's side. This is the kingdom of God in the form of grace, and hence in the concealment of the flesh. It is the kingdom of God as the kingdom of Christ.

But herein is also found the *menucha,* the place where God can rest in his work on earth. Everything is definitive in the Messiah.

And it has become clear to us in the Spirit (I Cor. 2:6, 10; II Cor. 1:22 — anointing; I John 2:20, 27). Here, too, clauses such as we have used above of the Messiah are in order. The clarity that is given us is a clarity exclusively *en pneúmati,* in the form of the indwelling *(inhabitatio)* of the Holy Spirit, in an unheard-of *epochê,* specifically the *epochê* of the ascension and the sacrament. All the same, whoever lives by the Spirit in the *mystérion* of the historical action of God in Jesus Christ can no longer have any doubts, any ultimate misunderstanding, about the meaning and glory of existence and the world in the plan of God.

At this point the whole of pneumatology, and hence the theory of religious and theological knowledge, should be worked out. We obviously cannot pursue these in this narrower context. I have made an attempt in this direction (a theory of knowledge on the basis not merely of Christology and the Scripture principle, but also of the outpouring and indwelling of the Holy Spirit) in *De vervulling van de wet.*

W. C. van Unnik, in his introduction to the translation of Gregory of Nyssa's *Oratio catechetica,* pp. 55-61, points out that Fathers use the word *mystérion* not only for the sacraments, but for all of

God's action in history, the whole time filled by the Spirit in and from Jesus Christ. I think we should return to the broad and deep use of the term, and therewith to this Christian pneumatological experience of history.

Compared with Jews and Gentiles, Christians are a third race, a race that has seen, with terror and joy, the lightning of God's Word and acts striking into history, a race that thus goes into the world with unparalleled courage in order that the apostolic Word may begin and complete its course.[4]

Thus, rightly understood, the Christian church really has to make something of the Old Testament. It is unquestionably the book of the people of Israel. This is a mystery of God that we must respect. But Israel does not have the final certainty and clarity needed to live in the world with the Word of God, that is, with the Old Testament.

This is particularly true because it was only in the Messiah and then in the Spirit that it became clear and certain that the promises and the kingdom of God — the things that are at issue in the Old Testament — are not identical to the people of Israel. Israel is no less a means than Jesus Christ. God's concern in Israel is with the nations and the world. This becomes basically clear and certain only with Jesus Christ's sending out of the disciples. It came about in an unquestionably strange and alien manner by way of the incarnation and rejection of the Messiah. But in this way it did in fact take place. Herein many of the intentions of the Old Testament were irrevocably fulfilled. The men of Israel cannot alter this, not even by repenting and turning to the Messiah.

The men of Israel might say that the nations of Western Europe incorporated little of the Torah and the kingdom of God into their culture and society. In this respect the apostolic process of Christianizing is often much like the history of the OT. They might also say that they are now building in Israel a state that will bear witness against all Christian nations. But they can hardly maintain that what has happened to the nations since the apostolate of Jesus Christ has been a meaningless blunder on the part of their God and ours. Nineteen hundred years of history cannot be so easily disposed of in the theological investigation of world reality.

That Israel is no less a means than Jesus Christ is a very different position from that of Barnabas, whose starting point is that the Jews lived in a misconception and had no inkling of the true spiritual purpose of the OT; cf. J. Klevinghaus, *Die theologische Stellung der apostolischen Väter*, pp. 20-32. Barnabas spiritualized the OT and legalized the gospel.

At this point we should recall anew that the statement that all the promises of God are Yea and Amen in Jesus Christ does not mean that every promise of God has Jesus Christ in view and thus is fulfilled in him. The issue is not so much Jesus Christ as the work that he came to do and did. In his work, however, the main concern is the kingdom of God, which acquired once and for all in him its *pied-à-terre*. This is why all the promises are Yea and Amen in him: they have in view the kingdom based on him and his work.

Legitimation and foundation thus stand in a remarkable dialectical relationship. The Old Testament legitimates Jesus as the Messiah, but this legitimation is also a foundation, namely, of his messiahship. And Jesus is the foundation of the Old Testament in respect of its main concern. This foundation again is a legitimation. Thus the one supports the other, the Old Testament and the gospel of Jesus Christ, and *vice versa*.

III

We encounter the same dialectic when we move on to the next point: that of *interpretation*.

The Old Testament is necessary for the Christian church because it interprets legitimately the gospel of Jesus Christ. In the words of H. W. Wolff, "for a full understanding of the Christ event between the Testaments, the Old Testament Word is just as necessary as the New Testament Word."[5] Or, as G. von Rad puts it, "our knowledge of Christ is incomplete without the Old Testament. The Old Testament, however, must first be heard in its witness to the Word of God, which creates history; and a Christ event may be discerned already in this Old Testament historical action of God — in his judgments no less than in his deliverances."[6] Without the Old Testament,

Jesus Christ cannot be understood in his kingship, which applies to the Gentiles too. To quote Wolff again: "The world sees incompletely, and to that degree incorrectly, the Christ who appeared in its midst if it does not recognize him, in the light of Old Testament expectation, as the fulfilment of the promised time of salvation."[7]

This indispensability of the Old Testament for the Christian church is true first of all in a purely historical sense. The ancient thesis that the New Testament can be understood historically only against the background of the Old Testament may be accepted as valid.

But there is also a deeper and fully theological sense in which the Old Testament is indispensable. "The structures of the Torah," Miskotte writes, "are without exception the presuppositions of the *kerygma,* the Christian message."[8] The Gentiles lose sight of the kingship in Jesus' messiahship if they do not interpret his gospel in the light of the Old Testament. For then they concentrate exclusively on his priestly work or on his person, in which the forgiving love of God comes to us, or on his ethical teaching and moral example, or on him as the great mystic, the soloist of the mystical choir of humanity.[9] But that he is King and *kyrios,* King of kings and Lord of lords, over the earth, even in political matters, is lost from view or spiritualized. The kingship of Jesus is clearly perceived to be the real point at issue when the gospel of Jesus Christ is understood, in the light of the Old Testament, as something utterly historical and hence also secular and earthly.

But difficulties arise again; for this interpretation in the light of the Old Testament is more than just interpretation. There is in it an element of supplementation. For in the New Testament it is none too clear that the cause of God in Jesus Christ is so purely historical, secular, earthly, theocratic, and political in intent. Whole periods and groups in the Christian church have been able at least to overlook this aspect and to interpret the indescribable gift as a super-added gift, an explanation of created life, or something that stands in *diastasis* alongside or in place of earthly reality (I have in mind here Roman Catholicism, Eastern Orthodoxy, Lutheranism, and

Anabaptism). The Reformed doctrine of sanctification and Kuyper's concept of the kingship of Christ over all spheres of life are the most earnest efforts toward this Old Testament interpretation of the gospel of Jesus Christ.[10]

Here again must we not use strict dialectic and say that the New Testament interprets the Old Testament as well as the Old the New? But the modalities that appear as soon as the kingdom of God is present as the kingdom of Christ force us to recognize that the Old Testament cannot be followed exactly in the Christian situation, that Christ in his own way corrects the Old Testament, and that this can be called an interpretation, again in the form of supplementation. But this interpretation and supplementation is not to be taken merely as a plus in relation to the Old Testament. The church is the suffering form of the kingdom of God, as Hoedemaker put it.[11] This is why he had more patience with the state than did Kuyper.

In any case contemporary exegesis invites systematic theology to reconsider seriously in its Christology the Old Testament data and perspectives that might serve to state theologically what is implied by saying that Jesus is Christ.[12] This could entail a revolution in dogmatics. I believe that the results of a full exegesis of the Old Testament might be healthier for the christological parties in doctrine and for dogmatics as a whole than the insights of modern christological dogmatics can ever be for the exegesis of the Old Testament.

Zimmerli writes: "The Old Testament does not fade into nothingness when fulfilled in Christ, though its special word is at an end. Christ is not fully understood unless integrated into the Old Testament word of promise in his kingship, though on the other hand he can be the only legitimate interpreter of the Old Testament promise in its abiding validity"; "Verheissung und Erfüllung," p. 54. Baumgärtel takes violent exception to this line of thought and will accept only an understanding and endorsement of the OT in terms of the NT; cf. *Verheissung,* pp. 114, 123.

That the interpretation of the OT in the light of the NT is a supplementation is missed by Luther in his understanding of the whole of the OT in Christian fashion and translation of it into Christian terms; cf. Bornkamm, *op. cit.,* pp. 86, 129-39, 185; Eng. tr., pp. 100f., 152-64, 219. In connection with the fact that this interpretation and supplementation are not to be taken merely as a plus in relation to the OT, the following ought to be noted:

(1) Christ's interpretation of the OT is linked with concentration on the expiation of guilt effected in the gospel.

(2) Compared with earthly politics, atonement and guilt have about them something spiritual and the messiahship of Jesus Christ is characterized by this spiritual element.

(3) This spiritual character of the gospel of Jesus Christ should not, however, be built up into an ontological dualism in which spiritual and earthly, religious and political, God and world, individual and society, or soul and body are hostile and antithetical as such.

(4) Thus, it is illegitimate to say that "Jesus Christ, the true Messiah-King, is the end of all the theocratic kingship and of the hierocracy peculiar to the Old Covenant"; Brunner, *Offenbarung und Vernunft*, pp. 122f.; Eng. tr., p. 105.

(5) Nor is it enough to say that "as Son of Man, second Adam, Jesus fulfils the destiny of man created by God; as the Servant of Yahweh he fulfils the history of his people. Both lines permit us to perceive that the entire history in which Christ effects salvation is connected with human sin"; Cullmann, *Christus und die Zeit*, p. 121; Eng. tr., p. 138. It must be remembered that the people Israel is especially the people of revelation by virtue of its learning the true meaning of human society and fellowship from God: it is the holy people under the true king, the servant of God and the shepherd of the people.

(6) The ministering of Jesus, who is Christ, does not stand in genuine antithesis to political ruling (love as the opposite of law and force), but it makes him so completely independent that this ministering becomes genuine ruling, and it thus becomes the reality and model of all true authority. Cf. J. H. Gunning, *De Eenheid des levens*, p. 64: "Anyone who lets himself be served even a little becomes oriented to the help of his servants. Only he who will not accept any more service at all, but serves himself at all points, is oriented to none, that is, has full dominion."

Kuyper commended the state to common grace on the one hand and to the power of (politically organized) Christians on the other. Hoedemaker believed the church must continue to serve the Word (which is more than simply preaching the gospel), especially in relation to the authorities, while the authorities (as such) must freely and independently decide what it means to live in the light of the Word of God.

IV

The fourth way of elucidating the Old Testament's necessity

for the Christian church, we have suggested, is the concept of *illustration.*

I am speaking here of more than the rich and profound world of Old Testament imagery, which is definitely necessary in preaching in order to give varied expression to what took place with and by Jesus Christ, what takes place with and by the *corpus Christi* and *corpus christianum,* and how a God-fearing man understands himself in the world and in the presence of God. All of this can be illustrated with endless variety by images drawn from the Old Testament. From the standpoint of technical homiletics these can hardly be dispensed with. A purely Christian preaching, restricting itself to the data of the New Testament and Christian tradition, would lack the warmth and color that the Old Testament imparts, by which preaching penetrates more deeply into the blood, into real life.[13]

This is all important enough. But the matter goes deeper. The language we use to express ourselves is more than a technical affair. This is true of the language of Canaan in which we proclaim the Messiah and the Spirit. The language impinges directly on life and truth.

In this context, however, illustration has to be understood in a much more profound sense. In fact, one can fully proclaim Jesus Christ *only* in the expressions and metaphors, concepts, and insights of the Old Testament. Why is this so? First of all, from the very outset he is the Messiah of Israel and only as such the Savior of the world. Second, he became what he did become on the way of crucifixion and resurrection only by essential implication in the problems in which Israel had entangled itself. Third, the question to which the work of Christ is particularly an answer — the question of guilt — is something wholly Old Testament in structure, since only Israel really knows what guilt is and in a certain sense bears guilt. Also, the answer that Jesus Christ is and gives in his work is expressed in the vocabulary of the Book of Leviticus,[14] so that one can never really master the gospel of the cross without working out in some way what is disparagingly called the Jewish theology of blood. Finally, the church itself, the body of Christ, the messenger and bearer of the gospel in the world, has always to take note of the great mystery that it is Israel in the sense that wild branches have been engrafted into the old stem, so that the preaching of the Christian church can and must draw on the Old Testament.

The primary reference of all this is to preaching, but it goes far beyond it. Thus, children of God can be directly related once they express themselves in the language of Canaan. But the Christianization of culture can succeed only to the degree that the cultural awareness is permeated by the basic structures of the Hebrew language and by the Old Testament, Israelitish manner of thought. Again, the possibility of the emergence of theology as a science depends on this Christianization of cultural awareness. (It is thus unnecessary to fall back on the thesis — which on my view is impossible from a Reformation standpoint — that the science of theology is a function of the church.) For the most distinctive feature of theology as a science is that, like philosophy, it is directed to ultimate truth, though it seeks to embrace this truth, not in abstract ideas, but in concrete historical facts. This is possible, however, only if man and society experience the world more or less after the manner of Israel.

K. H. Miskotte says that "Within the unity of Scripture the Old Testament has no validity of its own, but it does have independent significance. It cannot be understood in and of itself, but, taken up into one context with the New Testament, it has to set up signs that are independent — signs that encircle the one revelation and in their own peculiar way point to the present age of salvation"; "De prediking van het OT," p. 384; cf. also Miskotte, *Bijbelsch ABC,* esp. pp. 181f. O. Noordmans adds that the church is not yet able properly to speak the Pentecostal language of the kingdom of God; therefore it has to express itself in the language of the OT; "Het OT en de kerk," p. 106.

Because the children of God can be directly related once they express themselves in the language of Canaan, the problem of religious communication (Jaspers) is quite easily solved. This has always been of fundamental significance in relation to the question of fellowship in the church. In some ecclesiastical circles in Holland a very remarkable and important phenomenon may be discerned here.

V

This leads immediately to our fifth point — *historicization*. In every century the Old Testament has proved to be unreservedly necessary for the Christian church chiefly because it historicizes the gospel of Jesus in an essential way. I mean this in the true sense of the word. Only against the background and in the context of the Old Testament can it be maintained that Jesus Christ is an element in the history of God with Israel and consequently, as God's act, an historical fact.

In my view this must be taken with utmost seriousness and not transposed at once into the thought of "one revelation that is identical with Jesus Christ, or the *assumptio carnis,* the time of God, which also embraces human time, the eternal act of God, the one history that is above history" (K. H. Miskotte, "De prediking van het OT," pp. 376, 381). In terms of this thought I wrote in *Religie en politiek,* p. 128: "The biblical concept of history regards history rather as a circle; biblical history is the prophetic and apostolic witness that intersects in the fulness of time the true history of the incursion of revelation." This was a blunder that is now incomprehensible to me, and I hereby correct it.

Any child can see that historicity is the core of Christianity. No matter how great the scientific or (in particular) philosophical difficulties involved, in the intuition of the heart it is immediately apparent that all comfort and joy fade out of the gospel when one can no longer live by love as an historical reality.

Strange to say, theology through the centuries has had great difficulties with this historical core of the gospel. Contrary to its own nature,[15] it has continually sought to change this historical factuality into rationality by one means or another (doctrine, example, person, mystical conversion of human nature in its totality, the source that opens up a river of life, etc.).[16] But in preaching and in the hour of death every Christian, however unwillingly, returns to the cross of Golgotha, and to this alone.

Now it might be that this is not done only at the last but that an effort is made to do it — more after the manner of Christian love — in all thought and action. In such an attempt the Old Testament is indispensable, for it very plainly and unmistakably deals with pure history, though history in the full sense, since God and his speaking are the driving factors in it. In this light one is always forced to remember that we also have to do with history in the gospel of Jesus Christ. Here is a fully historical fact that is wholly God's act and for this reason salvation in the full sense: the person of Jesus Christ and his fate at Calvary.

In the kerygma of the bodily resurrection of Jesus Christ these elements are woven together with elemental power. Here history is so concentrated that one may ask whether the term history will do, or whether we ought to agree with G. van der Leeuw in speaking of "mythistory"[17] when the reference is to the deity of Jesus, the incarnation, the resurrection, and the ascension. There is much to be said in favor of this term. Who really believes it possible, for example, to embrace the person and self-consciousness of Jesus psychologically, anthropologically, and then also historically? To say things about primary and ultimate reality, about God, we are forced to speak in mythical language.

Dogma rightly does this when it describes Jesus as the Christ. But this does not mean that the gospel becomes a myth.[18] Dogma is simply trying to grasp the full content of the gospel. The gospel is no myth but mythistory. It is precisely when we try to engage in purely historical and anthropological exegesis, like Bultmann with his existential exegesis, that the gospel — and with it the Old Testament — is made into myth.[19]

Baumgärtel says that the real historicity of Jesus Christ is to be grounded, not in the OT, but exclusively in the incarnation; *Verheissung*, p. 113. In my view, however, history shows how easily the incarnation can be taken nonhistorically or in a limited historical sense or even metahistorically. In this connection it is pertinent to note that the author of the *Epistle of Barnabas*, on the basis of the historical Christ, does not refer the OT sacrifices allegorically to the broken heart, but typologically to the death of Christ, so that, in complete contradiction with his basic thought, he presupposes that they were genuinely and legitimately offered in the OT. Cf. on this J. Klevinghaus, *op. cit.*, p. 24 (cf. also pp. 106f. on the place of the law and the prophets in salvation history according to Ignatius).

We are as little able to understand psychologically and anthropologically the real depths of man apart from his relation to God, which is the true center of his life, as we are able to grasp the real nature of history without taking seriously the thought that every epoch is immediate to God.

VI

The Old Testament is also necessary for the Christian church in a very different way. This brings us to our sixth term. Along with historicization I have set *eschatologization*. This is, of course, only a word, but it is precisely adapted to express what I have in mind in this connection. The word "eschatologize" is meant to convey the fact that originally and finally, and hence continually, our concern is with God himself and the world in the naked subsistence of things.

This may be glimpsed at times in the New Testament, where it speaks of the end of faith, of the Son's giving of the kingdom to the Father, of the dwelling of God among men, of the new earth in which righteousness dwells, of the new birth of the world, of authority and the good as such (I Pet. 1:9; I Cor. 15:24, 28; Rev. 21:3; II Pet. 3:13; Matt. 19:28; Rom. 13:1-7). But generally speaking, this is all concealed in the particularity of revelation. The Messiah and the Spirit, the incarnation and the indwelling cover it over, keeping and preserving but also hiding it.

In the Old Testament this original and final element, this faithfulness to the earth and time, is more plainly visible. In my view this means that, in this respect, we have to speak most emphatically of the greater value of the Old Testament as compared with the New. The Old Testament has a more positive concern with creation and the kingdom, with the first things and the last, with the image and the law, with sanctification and humanity,[20] with ethos and culture, with society and marriage, with history and the state. These are precisely the matters at issue in the Old Testament. For this reason the Old Testament neither can nor should be expounded christologically, but only eschatologically, in other words *theocratically*. There is in it a profound confidence in the goodness of the world, the serviceability of man, and the possibility of sanctifying the earth.[21]

This the church needs for its own life, to keep it from hopeless entanglement in the problems of sin and atonement, as though only dark shadows lay on the earth and life. For God's sake it needs to be more human and secular than it has hitherto let itself be in its tradition.

One might well say with Brunner, "This act of representative suffering is to be His decisive word of revelation" (*Offenbarung und Vernunft*, p. 112; Eng. tr., p. 95), but this should not be taken to mean that in the expiation of sin the one true thing, the first and the last, is said and done. Protologically and eschatologically sin (and hence also atonement) is a secondary problem.

It was Luther who, in his experience of the OT, found that the law torments us with guilt and death; Bornkamm, *op. cit.*, p. 123; Eng. tr., pp. 144f. Baumgärtel thinks that along these lines the OT is predominantly of negative significance for the Christian experience, so that life is darkened and the whole world brought under a shadow. Such a view of the OT seems to me to be affected by the experience of the medieval monk; in consequence, the problem of the OT has been set today in a completely mistaken light. Cf. Baumgärtel, *Verheissung*, p. 141.

For the consciousness of the Christian church throughout the centuries there has always been a surplus in the Old Testament that it could not assimilate.[22] This surplus is not just the cultus. The church has spiritualized this or brought it into its own liturgy or used it as a witness to the message of Golgotha or simply said that it has been superseded by Christ. In my view, however, we touch the nerve of the problem once we assert that Christian life is fundamentally structured cultically, inasmuch as it stands in a circle around the great sacrificial work of God at Calvary, where the means of salvation became the fact of salvation, and the cultus became wholly history and history became wholly cultic. In this case, however, there is hardly any cause to ask whether the Old Testament cultus is superfluous for the Christian church.

The only point is that the surplus is also to be found in the social ideal of the Old Testament, a just society, the brotherhood of all men, the king or authority who is the true shepherd — not God on earth but the servant of God. For centuries the Christian church has ignored these things or acted as if they were adequately achieved in the fellowship of the community, as though the harsh realities of social and economic life, of domestic and foreign politics, could be kept off the horizon of the Christian church and its God, as though the cross of Christ were not and did not have to be set up especially in these realities.[23]

Baumgärtel is right to say that "in the old covenant the individual is fundamentally only a member of the people of Israel in its relation to God"; op. cit., p. 40. But he sees this as part of the limitation "with which the Old Testament understands the basic promise." P. Volz points out, however, that this element is most important for the health of religious life, with its dangers of individualism, inwardness, and self-seeking, and then says: "These two things — the idea of community and the public character of religion — have largely perished from our individualistic religion and must be won back again from the Old Testament"; Mose und sein Werk, p. 79. One cannot be permeated enough by the significance of the basic fact that a Torah is the core of OT revelation, and that this is oriented to the community and the common life of the holy people, just as the Messiah is expected primarily as a king, again with a view to the community and the common life. At this point the exact labors of many exegetes seem to be impotent, and the dogmatic standpoint, namely, that in relation to God the individual life of man is far more important than the corporate life, exercises a crushing affect.

Von Rad has made an important attempt to escape religious and Christian individualism; cf. "Verheissung," p. 411. In so doing he has called attention to the significance of the OT for the church. Baumgärtel is obviously unable to make anything of this observation; "Der Dissensus," pp. 306f. This is obviously because of his dogmatic stance. In his ecclesiology the church is regarded wholly in terms of the individual Christian. For the rest, I do not think that Von Rad is wholly right. In order truly to understand and exploit the social ideal of the OT, one must go beyond the corpus Christi to the corpus christianum.

The Old Testament draws our attention to this. But in so doing it undoubtedly goes a step further than the New Testament. To put it even more sharply, the New Testament is not enough. It leaves us in the lurch in respect of life in society on earth and in time. One may then appeal to natural law, but what is really needed is to go back to the Old Testament. This is where the Old Testament has its own independent significance for the Christian church. One can still accommodate and accept here the notion that the Old Testament is God's picture-book, the source of elements of piety and knowledge of God. Even an existential interpretation of the Old Testament, an attempt to fathom human life with the aid of Old Testament passages, can have a definite — if limited — place from this standpoint.[24] But the quintessence is to be found in politics in the broadest sense of the term: the state, social and economic life, culture — in a word, the sanctification of the earth.

In my view Martin Buber is completely correct to level against the Christian church throughout the centuries the accusation that it has never really been faithful to this Old Testament belief, this grand vision of the God of Israel, this visionary faith in the possibility of the sanctification of the earth.[25] From the necessity of the cross of Christ, which the church has accepted on the basis of the New Testament, the false conclusion has been drawn that no more can be made of the earth. There has arisen a false belief in death.

Obbink says that "the Old Testament offers much more material for the knowledge of God than the New Testament. . . . We not only need the Old Testament to be able truly to understand the New Testament, we also need it to learn who God is"; *Theologische bezinning op het OT*, p. 30. The same insight may be found in Edelkoort, *Karaktertrekken*, p. 21. K. H. Miskotte reacts against this idea with the outburst: "If [someone] says that the Old Testament, while bearing no 'witness to Christ,' contains 'witness to God,' the question arises as to what is understood in God's name and by 'God' "; "De prediking van het OT," p. 368. Obviously, his whole dogmatic system lies behind this reaction.

Baumgärtel lets slip the qualifier ". . . which like every divine requirement cannot be put into practice in the empirical world"; *Verheissung*, p. 58. As I see it, this statement is based on a Lutheran dogmatic system rather than the Bible.

Here, then, two deeply probing questions must be put.
(1) Can the church really proceed on the assumption that its preaching must be exclusively preaching of Christ? If it does, is it not overlooking the fact that Christ came for the sake of the kingdom? And does this not imply that its preaching must continually open itself up in all its aspects to the preaching of the kingdom? Only thus can the Old Testament have a legitimate function in the church, whether exegetically or homiletically. Only thus can it have such a function as the distinct and independent canonical Word of God.

Obbink's observation is important: the kingdom of God is not something we later find in the OT only after we read it in terms of the NT; it is already wholly present in the OT; *Theologische bezinning op het OT*, pp. 27ff.
Here the great problem of the relation between the OT and natural law arises again. Luther divides the OT into *natural* law and *national* law. The latter is binding only on Israel, and the nations of the earth neither have nor will have anything whatever to do with it; cf. Bornkamm, *Luther und das AT*, pp. 105-11; Eng. tr., pp. 120-29. Newer insights into the connection between law and covenant, the order of national life and revelation, ought to make us rather more cautious in the face of this radical and simple solution to the problem, particularly since the problem of natural law is by no means simple in itself.

(2) What does the Christian church do when it has acknowledged the Old Testament as the canon? Does it bind the Old Testament to itself? Throughout the centuries it looks suspiciously as though this is what has happened. As soon as the attempt is made to expound the Old Testament with a view to, or in the light of, the church's proclamation of Christ, this terrible risk is incurred. In face of it what should be done is to abide by the fact, with all its implications, that the church's recognition of the canon of the Old Testament can mean only that it binds itself to the Old Testament, and never *vice versa*. The basis for this is already found in the fundamental concepts of the Reformation doctrine of Scripture. The Roman Catholic Church, controlled by its doctrine of the authoritative exposition of Scripture by the church, can handle the Old Testament

with great freedom, not to mention caprice. From the Reformation standpoint, however, acknowledgment of the Old Testament means that we are bound fast to it. This may eventually be a heavy burden. There is always a desire to set aside the Old Testament, as Harnack did in principle, and as many do in practice when they no longer preach the Old Testament. It is to be regarded as a blessing that (at least in Reformed Christianity) the preaching of the Christian church has always drawn willingly from the well of the Old Testament. But it has to be the whole Old Testament, as God's own Word, that is allowed to speak this way in the modern world.

We cannot accept Bornkamm's comparison of the Puritans, who used figures from the OT to illustrate the world of their time and their own destiny, with Luther, who is supposed to have done the very opposite — projected his struggles into the OT. Bornkamm concludes that there is a plain distinction here between "creative spirit and artificial reconstruction" and between "freedom in handling Scripture in Christ and biblicism"; *op. cit.*, p. 23; Eng. tr., p. 27. In this judgment there is no adequate recognition of the seriousness of the problem of the OT as canon in the modern age.

These then are the six ways in which the necessity and indispensability of the Old Testament for the Christian church must be argued.

VII

Two problems remain, however, and we can only outline these in closing.

First is the problem of the Old Testament as a special canon in the Christian church. It is most remarkable that the Christian church has two canons. Surely this will cause confusion similar to that of having two captains on one ship.

Or is it incorrect to say that there are two canons? Should we put it more cautiously (or, as one might say, less bluntly) and say that, instead of two canons, there is one double canon? But such a formulation hardly makes things much clearer. Should we then go further and state that, instead of two canons or one double canon, there is only the one canon of Old

and New Testament together? Kohlbrügge supports this view
when he points out that to differentiate too sharply between
the Old and New Testaments would be unbiblical. One should
speak, not of a duality, but rather of a plurality in the canonical
Word of God, that of the law, the prophets, the evangelists,
and the apostles.[26] Not so pertinent in this connection is the
fact that these became canonical at various times in history and
were woven together into a single whole.

This solution is less self-evident, however, when we consider that the agent of canonization is different in the two cases,
Judaism in the case of the Old Testament, the Christian community in the case of the New. These are certainly not the
same. There are also certain difficulties behind this state of
affairs.

What did the canonization of the New Testament really
involve? We have said that the New Testament regards itself
as fully legitimated by the Old. But in canonization the New
Testament itself becomes a legitimating authority. One could
hardly argue otherwise in view of its incongruity with the Old
Testament.

But if there is only one canon, has the New Testament
simply been taken up and integrated into the Old?

Or is there only one canon in the sense that the Old Testament alone is the canon and the New has just been added at
the end as an explanatory glossary? — explanatory in the two-
fold sense of interpretation and validation, yet obviously also
in the sense that this interpretation and endorsement of the
canon is, for its part, also recognized as canon.[27]

We might point out that even Calvin in his commentary on II
Tim. 3:17 speaks of the NT as an appendix *(accessio)* in the two-
fold sense of exposition and ratification *(explicationem una cum
rerum exhibitione).*

Or is the reverse true, namely, that there is only one canon,
but the Christian church must seek this in the New Testament,
so that the Old Testament enters in only as horizon and background?

How is this strange problem to be interpreted systematically?

We cannot solve this problem here. This could be done only in the much more comprehensive context of the whole problem of Scripture and canon. It is not advisable to try to force a solution to this interesting and exciting question, for our deliberations on the Old Testament and its exegesis, Christ in the Old Testament, and the necessity of the Old Testament for the Christian church have surely made it apparent that the whole problem of the Old Testament, and with it, in my view, its place as canon, needs to be thought out afresh. Historico-critical investigation has opened our eyes to the fact that in the course of the centuries the Christian church has treated the Old Testament just as uncertainly and unsuitably as it has treated the Jews.

One can at least say, however, that the problem of authority in the Christian faith, as perceived also in the question of the canon, can be resolved to some degree only when one is prepared to recognize in principle a plurality of courts. No flat unity or absoluteness can be achieved. We are stuck with manifoldness. This is in keeping with the nature of love. God's cause, too, is still on the march.

In what is said above I have not taken into account the possibilities opened up by the non-Reformed intuition that the OT alone is Holy Scripture and that the NT is by nature oral *kerygma*. This is a very important, but very difficult, thought. Properly to evaluate it, one would have to raise anew the whole problem of tradition. Modern systematic theology has, off and on, devoted much attention to this concept; cf. for example H. Diem, *Das Problem des Schriftkanons;* but one cannot possibly say that contemporary Protestantism has at its disposal a theology into which the concept can be even partially integrated.

I have discussed the plurality of authorities functioning in the Christian faith in my essay "Het gezag in de kerk." In my view the plurality of authorities is essential not merely because there is an indissoluble duality between God and man but also because truth takes place in the movement of time. Truth, then, is not yet complete. The living God is still on the march with his human children. In regard to the present problem this means that one should not force the duality of OT and NT into a unity.

Secondly, we may refer to a problem that brings this out

even more clearly, namely, that of the Old Testament as the book of the people Israel.

Today this problem has come into view in completely new contexts and structures. Hence I can present only the outlines of it.

On the one hand the Christian church must cling to the fact that the Old Testament too has become valid and plain for the Gentiles through and with Jesus Christ.[28] For many reasons one cannot have the New Testament and the gospel of Jesus Christ without at the same time, and always, having the Old Testament as well. On the other hand, however, it has become awkward and surprising for us in modern times that the people of Israel is still here. The real theological problem is *in what way* it still exists. But the *factual* existence of the Jews, the synagogue, and particularly the State of Israel,[29] presents us with facts that are *theologically* relevant.

This seems to me to be directly apparent today. The terrible persecutions to which the Jews were subjected in the most serious crisis in Christianized Western culture, that is, Nazism, have surely opened our eyes to it. We have thus been given a glimpse of the wealth and depth of the Jewish religious experience of the world, of the enormous contribution the Jewish spirit has made to world culture, and of Judaism's conception of universal unity in relation to the future of the human race. As though that were not enough, there has come also the great surprise of the establishment and development of the State of Israel. Anyone who seeks truth in the strict sense theologically and not just philosophically, so that he is ready to find it not merely in abstract and absolute principles, but rather in concrete historical facts, will not simply set these things aside as though it were childish fantasy to think that God has had a hand in what has happened.

But has God really had a hand in it? In respect of the gospel the Jews are God's enemies, though in respect of the election they are loved by him. This is what Paul said about the Jews of his day. Have things happened since then that force us to say that this is not true of the Jews of our time? But what is meant by this love of God controlled by the election? Does

God still have something for Israel in his world plan? Here more than anywhere else it would be advisable to pronounce a theological *non liquet*. To say that one knows what God has for his people Israel would be arrogant anticipation. To say that one can see that God has nothing more for Israel might well contradict Scripture.

While such a *non liquet* is justifiable in respect of the place of the Jews in God's plan for the world, we must come to some decision now on the question of how the Old Testament is to be regarded, whether as the book of the Christian church alone, or as still and always the book of the people Israel too.

In this decision room must certainly be found for the idea that all the apostolic work of the Christian church among the Jews must be conducted from the decisive standpoint that it is a conversation with Israel. Only here — in relation to Israel — may the Christian church use the maieutic method, which presupposes that the truth is already in the partner in the discussion and has only to be brought out of him by discussion or dialogue. The truth is in Israel: it has the Old Testament.

The new church order of the Reformed Church of the Netherlands speaks expressly in Article VII of conversation with Israel, and it gives this precedence as the first aspect of the church's apostolate. Only then follow missionary work, evangelism, and Christianization as further aspects.

Nevertheless, a certain irresolution overtakes us at this point. Can the truth for which the Christian church stands, can Jesus as the Messiah, be brought out of the people of Israel — that is, out of the Old Testament — simply by dialogue? Do we trust ourselves as the Christian church to be able to show the Jews from the Old Testament that Jesus is Christ? Or would we rather take our position exclusively in the New Testament? Then the conversation becomes pure witness. It is narrated of Philip, however, that he used an Old Testament text when he preached to the Ethiopian eunuch (Acts 8:35).

If we are undecided about what to do here, a new doubt arises about the further question of whether the Old Testament can be interpreted in any other way than that found in the New

Testament. One might think, for example, of the Talmud or modern Jewish religious philosophy. It is immediately apparent that this is a real historical possibility. Whether it is also historically legitimate, that is, historical in the full sense, whether it will also stand up theologically, is the question that impresses itself on us with such urgency.

Israel appeals to the Old Testament and bases itself upon it. How is this to be evaluated in the light of God, of God as we know him from the Old and New Testaments in their unity and incongruity? Is the Old Testament, in one way or another, still the book of Israel as well? This question can be answered only in a wider context. An answer can be given only in connection with the question of the theological significance of Judaism in the context of history as God's history with the world. Hence it cannot be sought here.

In our consideration of the Old Testament as a special canon in the Christian church we have ended with the problem of Scripture and its canonical authority. The question whether the Old Testament is the book of the people of Israel narrows down strictly to the question of the catholicity of the church. Does everything end in the church? Does everything, not only Israel, but history and creation, exist for the sake of the church? Or is the church only one among many forms of the kingdom of God, and does its catholicity consist precisely in the fact that it respects, acknowledges, and holds dear all forms of the kingdom, for example, even the people of Israel?

Thus our discussion of the problems of the Old Testament ends with two of the great themes of theology — canonical Scripture and the catholic church.

Footnotes to Chapter Three

[1] Strathmann points out that this has normative and validating rather than prophetic significance; *TWNT,* IV, 501; *TDNT,* IV, 497.

[2] In his commentary *ad loc.,* Calvin even thinks that the whole problem of the authority of the Christian faith is rooted in this appeal to the OT by Jesus. Cf. Schroten, *Christus, de middelaar,* pp. 304-09.

[3] This formulation is taken from the sacramental teaching of the Belgic Confession, Article 33: "Therefore the signs are not empty or meaningless, so as to deceive us. For Jesus Christ is the true object presented by

them [*Iesum Christum ... pro sua veritate habent*], without whom they would be of no moment."

[4]Stauffer, *Die Theologie des NT*, pp. 30-33.

[5]Wolff, "Der grosse Jesreeltag," p. 102.

[6]Von Rad, "Typologische Auslegung," p. 33.

[7]Wolff, "Der grosse Jesreeltag," p. 103.

[8]Miskotte, *Edda en Thora*, p. 385.

[9]Van Ruusbrooc, *Van VII trappen in den graed der gheesteleker minnen, Werken*, III, 262.

[10]A recent reaction of Lutheranism to this serious effort, which makes sense from a biblical and even a NT standpoint, may be found in Künneth's *Politik zwischen Dämon und Gott*, pp. 516-41.

[11]Cf. Chapter Two, note 19, p. 73.

[12]Cf. Zimmerli, "Verheissung und Erfüllung," pp. 57f.

[13]Cf. Bornkamm, *Luther und das AT*, pp. 9-37; Eng. tr., pp. 11-44: "The Old Testament as Mirror of Life."

[14]Gispen, *De Christus in het OT*, pp. 13ff.

[15]Cf. Köhler, *Dogmengeschichte*, I, 54.

[16]Bergema states that "Just as the New Testament keeps us from interpreting the Old Testament legalistically, so the Old Testament prevents us from understanding the New Testament idealistically or mystically after the Greek manner"; "Het OT en de zending," p. 120.

[17]Van der Leeuw, *De primitieve mensch en de religie*, p. 182.

[18]Zimmerli, *op. cit.*, p. 54.

[19]*Ibid.*, p. 57.

[20]Vriezen emphasizes that the OT is the source of all thoughts of pure humanity; *Hoofdlijnen der theologie van het OT*, p. 147.

[21]It thus sounds strange and wrong when the OT situation is described as a state of humiliation; cf. P. J. Roscam Abbing, *Diakonia*, pp. 103f.

[22]Koole, *De overname*, pp. 77ff.

[23]This may be seen especially on the mission fields; cf. Freytag, *Die junge Christenheit*, p. 202; Eng. tr., p. 196: "But it is noticeable that the Old Testament performs a special mission in the inner life of immature Christianity."

[24]Wolff, "Der grosse Jesreeltag," p. 101; De Wilde, *Het probleem van het OT*, pp. 24f.

[25]Cf. Buber's *An der Wende*.

[26]Kohlbrügge, *loc. cit.*

[27]Cf. Chapter Two, note 45, p. 74.

[28]Wolff, *op. cit.*, pp. 100, 102.

[29]Zimmerli, "Verheissung und Erfüllung," pp. 58f.

H2801

LIST OF WORKS CITED

Barth, Karl. *Das Bekenntnis der Reformation und unser Bekennen.* Munich, 1935.
———. *Kirchliche Dogmatik,* Volume II, Part 2, and Volume IV, Part 1. Zurich, 1940, 1953. English translation, *Church Dogmatics.* Edinburgh, 1957, 1956.
Baumgärtel, F. "Der Dissensus im Verständnis des Alten Testaments." *Evangelische Theologie,* July-August 1954.
———. "Ohne Schlüssel vor der Tür des Wortes Gottes?" *Evangelische Theologie,* December 1953.
———. *Verheissung. Zur Frage des evangelischen Verständnisses des Alten Testaments.* Gütersloh, 1952.
Bergema, H. "Het Oude Testament en de zending." *Vox theologica,* March 1938.
Berkouwer, G. C. *De triomf der genade in de theologie van Karl Barth.* Kampen, 1954. English translation, *The Triumph of Grace in the Theology of Karl Barth* (tr. Harry R. Boer). Grand Rapids, 1956.
———. *Het werk van Christus.* Kampen, 1953. English translation, *The Work of Christ* (tr. C. Lambregtse). Grand Rapids, 1965.
Blauw, J. *Goden en Menschen. Plaats en betekenis van de heidenen in de Heilige Schrift.* Groningen, 1950.
Bornkamm, H. *Luther und das Alte Testament.* Tübingen, 1948. English translation, *Luther and the Old Testament* (tr. Ruth and Eric Gritsch). Philadelphia, 1969.
Braun, J. "Altes Testament," "Reich Gottes," "Testament," in *Handbuch der katholischen Dogmatik.* Freiburg, 1926.
Brouwer, A. M. *De Bergrede.* Zeist, 1930.
Brunner, E. *Dogmatik,* Volume I. Zurich, 1946. English translation, *The Christian Doctrine of God* (tr. Olive Wyon). Philadelphia, 1950.
———. *Offenbarung und Vernunft.* Zurich, 1961². English translation, *Revelation and Reason* (tr. Olive Wyon). Philadelphia, 1946.
Buber, Martin. *An der Wende. Reden über das Judentum.* Cologne-Olten, 1952. English translation, *At the Turning: Three Essays on Judaism.* New York, 1952.
Bultmann, R. "Weissagung und Erfüllung," in *Glauben und Verstehen,* II. Tübingen, 1952. Pp. 162-86. English translation, "Prophecy and Fulfilment," in *Essays: Philosophical and Theological* (tr. James C. G. Greig). London, 1955. Pp. 182-208.

Cullmann, Oscar. *Christus und die Zeit.* Zurich, 1946. English translation, *Christ and Time* (tr. Floyd V. Filson). Philadelphia, 1950.

Diem, H. *Das Problem des Schriftkanons.* Zurich, 1952.
——. *Theologie als kirchliche Wissenschaft,* Volume I. Munich, 1951.
Diestel, L. *Geschichte des Alten Testaments in der christlichen Kirche.* Jena, 1869.
Edelkoort, A. H. *Karaktertrekken der oudtestamentische religie.* Amsterdam, 1945.
——. "De motieven van den strijd tegen het Jodendom." *Vox theologica,* March 1938.
Eichrodt, W. *Theologie des Alten Testaments,* Volume I. Leipzig, 1939. English translation, *Theology of the Old Testament* (tr. J. Baker). Philadelphia, 1961.
Fiolet, A., O.F.M. *Een kerk in onrust om haar belijdenis.* Nijkerk, 1953.
Freytag, W. *Die junge Christenheit im Umbruch des Ostens.* Berlin, 1938. English translation, *Spiritual Revolution in the East* (tr. L. M. Stalker). London, 1940.
Genderen, J. van. *Herman Witsius: bijdrage tot de kennis der gereformeerde theologie.* The Hague, 1953.
Gispen, W. H. *De Christus in het Oude Testament.* Delft, 1952.
Goppelt, L. *Typos. Die typologische Deutung des Alten Testaments im Neuen.* Gütersloh, 1939.
Groot, J. de. *De Psalmen: Verstaat gij wat gij leest?* Baarn, 1941.
Gunning, J. H. *De eenheid des Levens.* Nijmegen, 1903.

Haitjema, T. L. *De richtingen in de Nederlandse Hervormde Kerk.* Wageningen, n. d.
Harnack, A. *Marcion: Das Evangelium vom fremden Gott.* Leipzig, 1924.
Hellbardt, H. "Christus, das Telos des Gesetzes," *Evangelische Theologie,* September 1936.
Heppe, H. *Die Dogmatik der evangelischen-reformierten Kirche.* Elberfeld, 1861. English translation, *Reformed Dogmatics* (tr. G. T. Thomson). London, 1950.
Héring, J. *La première épître de Saint Paul aux Corinthiens.* Neuchâtel-Paris, 1949. English translation, *The First Epistle of St. Paul to the Corinthians* (tr. A. W. Heathcote and P. J. Allcock). London, 1962.
Hirsch, E. *Das Alte Testament und die Predigt des Evangeliums.* Tübingen, 1936.
Hoedemaker, P. J. *Handboek voor het Nieuwe Testament.* Amsterdam, 1906.
——. *Handboek voor het onderwijs in het Oude Testament.* Amsterdam, n.d.
Honders, H. J. *Andreas Rivetus als invloedrijk gereformeerde theoloog in Holland's bloeitijd.* The Hague, 1930.
Huizinga, J. *De wetenschap der geschiedenis.* Haarlem, 1937.
Hulst, A. R. *Hoe moeten wij het Oude Testament uitleggen?* Wageningen, 1941.

Klevinghaus, J. *Die Theologische Stellung der apostolischen Väter zur alttestamentliche Offenbarung.* Gütersloh, 1948.

Kohlbrügge, H. F. *Wozu das Alte Testament?* Elberfeld, 1855.

Köhler, W. *Dogmengeschichte als Geschichte des christlichen Selbstbewusstseins.* Zurich, 1951.

Koole, J. L. *De overname van het Oude Testament door de christelijke kerk.* Hilversum, 1938.

Koopmans, J. *Het oudkerkelijke dogma in de Reformatie, bepaaldelijk bij Calvijn.* Wageningen, 1938.

Korff, F. W. A. *Het christelijk geloof en de niet-christelijke godsdiensten.* Amsterdam, 1946.

———. *Christologie. De leer van het komen Gods.* Nijkerk, 1941.

Kraus, H. J. "Gespräch mit Martin Buber." *Evangelische Theologie,* July-August 1952.

Kühler, W. J. *Geschiedenis der Nederlandsche Doopsgezinden in de zestiende eeuw.* Haarlem, 1932.

Künneth, W. *Politik zwischen Dämon und Gott. Eine christliche Ethik des Politischen.* Berlin, 1954.

Kuyper, A. *Uit het Woord.* Amsterdam, 1884.

Leeuw, G. van der. *De primitieve mensch en de religie.* Groningen-Batavia, 1937.

Lodensteyn, J. van. *Beschouwinge van Zion.* Utrecht, 1683.

Miskotte, K. H. *Bijbelsch ABC.* Nijkerk, n.d.

———. *Edda en thora. Een vergelijking van germaansche en israelitische religie.* Nijkerk, n.d.

———. "De prediking van het Oude Testament," in *Handboek voor de prediking.* Amsterdam, 1948.

———. *Het wezen der joodsche religie.* Amsterdam, 1933.

Niftrik, G. C. van. "De verborgen zin der Schrift," in *Schrift en kerk.* Nijkerk, 1953.

Noordmans, O. "Het Oude Testament en de kerk," in *Zoeklichten.* Amsterdam, 1949.

Noth, M. "Die Vergegenwärtigung des Alten Testaments in der Verkündigung." *Evangelische Theologie,* July-August 1952.

Obbink, H. W. *Theologische bezinning op het Oude Testament.* Nijkerk, 1942.

Oosterhoff, B. J. *Het openbaringskarakter van het Oude Testament.* Alphen aan den Rijn, 1954.

Rad, Gerhard von. "Predigt über Ruth, I." *Evangelische Theologie,* July-August 1952.

———. "Typologische Auslegung des Alten Testaments." *Evangelische Theologie,* July-August 1952.

———. "Verheissung." *Evangelische Theologie,* December 1953.

Roessingh, K. H. "De moderne theologie in Nederland," in *Verzamelde Werken.* Arnheim, 1930.

Roscam Abbing, P. J. *Diakonia.* The Hague, 1950.

———. "De kerk en het Oude Testament," in *Schrift en kerk.* Nijkerk, 1953.

Rowley, H. H. *The Relevance of the Bible.* New York, 1944.

42801

Ruler, A. A. van. "De bevinding in de prediking," in *Schrift en kerk*. Nijkerk, 1953.
——. "Het gezag in de kerk." *Wending*, June 1953.
——. *Religie en politiek*. Nijkerk, 1945.
——. "Theologie des Apostolates." *Evangelische Missionszeitung*, March 1954. (Also in *Mission — heute!* Bethel, 1954. Pp. 13-33.
——. *De vervulling van de wet*. Nijkerk, 1947.
Ruusbrooc, Jan van. *Van VII trappen in den graed der gheesteleker minnen*, III. Tielt, 1947.

Scheers, G. P. *Philippus Jacobus Hoedemaker*. Wageningen, 1939.
Schleiermacher, F. *Der christliche Glaube nach den Grundsätzen der evangelischen Kirche im Zusammenhang dargestellt*. English translation, *The Christian Faith* (ed. H. R. Mackintosh and M. S. Stewart). Edinburgh, 1928.
Schoeps, H. J. In *Theologische Literaturzeitung*, February 1954.
Schrenk, G. *Gottesreich und Bund im älteren Protestantismus*. Gütersloh, 1923.
Schroten, H. *Christus, de middelaar, bij Calvin*. Utrecht, 1948.
Sellin, E. "Beurteilung und Verwendung des AT in der christlichen Kirche," in *Die Religion in Geschichte und Gegenwart*, I², 982-985.
Sepp, C. *Proeve eener pragmatische geschiedenis der theologie in Nederland van 1787 tot 1858*. Amsterdam, 1860.
Sevenster, G. *De Christologie van het Nieuwe Testament*. Amsterdam, 1946.
Snijders, G. *Friedrich Adolph Lampe*. Harderwijk, 1954.
Stange, C. *Dogmatik*. Gütersloh, 1927.
Stauffer, E. *Die Theologie des Neuen Testaments*. Gütersloh, 1948⁴. English translation, *New Testament Theology* (tr. John Marsh). New York, 1955.

Unnik, W. C. van. "Introduction" to Gregory of Nyssa's *Oratio catechetica*. Amsterdam, 1949.

Valeton, J. J. P., Jr., *Het Oude Testament en de "critiek"*. Baarn, 1906.
Vischer, Wilhelm. *Das Christuszeugnis des Alten Testaments*. Zurich, 1946. English translation, *The Witness of the Old Testament to Christ* (tr. A. B. Crabtree). London, 1949.
Volz, P. *Mose und sein Werk*. Tübingen, 1932.
Vriezen, T. C. *Hoofdlijnen der theologie van het Oude Testament*. Wageningen, 1949¹.

Wilde, W. J. de. *Het probleem van het Oude Testament*. Nijkerk, n.d.
——. *Het profetische getuigenis*. Amsterdam, 1949.
Wolff, H. W. "Der grosse Jesreeltag." *Evangelische Theologie*, July-August 1952.

Zimmerli, W. "Verheissung und Erfüllung." *Evangelische Theologie*, July-August 1952.